BURNING MONEY

J. Peter Grace

BURNING MONEY

The Waste of Your Tax Dollars

Macmillan Publishing Company

New York

Collier Macmillan Publishers

London

Macmillan Publishing Company
866 Third Avenue, New York, N.Y. 10022
Collier Macmillan Canada, Inc.

Library of Congress Cataloging in Publication Data
Grace, J. Peter (Joseph Peter)
  Burning money.
  Includes indexes.
  1. Waste in government spending—United States.
2. United States—Appropriations and expenditures.
3. United States—Executive departments—Management.
I. Title.
HJ2052.G68   1984   353.0072   84-15493
ISBN 0-02-544930-3

Macmillan books are available at special discounts for
bulk purchases for sales promotions, premiums, fund-raising,
or educational use. Special editions or book excerpts
can also be created to specification.
For details, contact:

    Special Sales Director
    Macmillan Publishing Company
    866 Third Avenue
    New York, New York 10022

10 9 8 7 6 5 4 3 2 1

Designed by Jack Meserole

Printed in the United States of America

To the nation's 82 million taxpayers,
the true victims of government waste

Contents

BURNING MONEY

Chapter 1

A Billion Here, a Billion There . . .

Did You Hear the One about the Dishpan Hands?

Most people think that government is a rather boring subject. Absolutely nothing could be further from the truth. In fact, the government in some respects is a veritable treasure-house of one-liners. Lurking between the pages of many a seemingly stale government report is the kind of hilarious raw material that any stand-up comedian would give his eyeteeth to get hold of—material that would leave the audience rolling in the aisles. Unfortunately, in the government's comedy routine it's usually the taxpayer who plays the unwitting straight man. Here is an example:

A Federal government dishwasher approaches her supervisor and complains that the rinse water is too hot, much too hot, for her hands. So she has decided that frankly she just can't continue in the dishwashing profession unless something drastic is done at once.

Alright, says the supervisor, we'll get you rubber gloves. The dishwasher tries out her new rubber gloves, but soon returns to her supervisor, this time complaining that the gloves irritate her skin. Now do you assume that this luckless employee was transferred to some other sort of work? Ah, then you don't understand the government's ways.

No, this victim of dishpan hands was instead classified as

permanently "disabled," thus entitled to collect full on-the-job disability pay—for the rest of her life. She can go soak those unfortunate dishpan hands in the soothing waters of Acapulco Bay, while the rest of us are working hard to support her with our tax dollars.

An isolated incident of government foolishness, you might think. Just an amusing fluke. Unfortunately, it is no fluke. In fact, that "disabled" dishwasher is symptomatic of the unbelievably wasteful and irrational policies and practices of the Federal government. You see, a Civil Service worker is eligible for disability retirement at any age after five years on the job if he or she is unable to perform any one "essential function" of that current job. (Many jobs involve dozens of "essential functions.") There's no such thing as partial disability in the Federal government, as there is in private industry. Now, this is not to say that all Federal employees, in particular those who are granted disability retirement, are slackers. They are just acting within the limits and standards of Federal employment.

Result? Incentives are incentives. We all respond to them. The case of the "disabling" dishpan hands is not an isolated incident, but rather is repeated over and over in Federal employment. Civil Service workers between the ages of 30 and 50 are 50 percent more likely to file disability retirement claims than workers in the private sector, for the water runneth hot in Washington, D.C., and those government desks, one imagines, have razor-sharp edges. Perhaps we should count our blessings. If the seat of our Federal government were located in Butte, Montana, or Bangor, Maine, we'd probably be paying Civil Service disability retirement for frostbite and windburn. At the end of fiscal 1982, more than a third of a million former Civil Service workers were receiving annual disability benefits of about $3.5 billion. Of course, some of the recipients are doubtless truly disabled. But how many cases of dishpan hands are on the rolls, too?

A study found one Civil Service disability pay recipient running a pizza parlor; another nursing his "disability" behind the counter of a flower shop; and a third operating her own ceramics shop (this poor former public servant was getting disability benefits for an elbow injury which, while precluding Federal employment, did not seem to prevent her from fashioning ceramics).

Of course, living on Civil Service disability retirement isn't everyone's idea of The Big Score. To really live high, you could get a grant from a little-known government entity called the Minority Business Development Agency. An Inspector General's report found, for example, that one recipient of a $4 million MBDA grant rented two cars and a townhouse, bought unauthorized gifts, promoted "questionable activities," and, to top it all off, forgot to pay $315,000 in taxes, fees, and salaries.

Then there was a contractor for the National Institute of Education who managed to do quite well at taxpayer expense. How? Let us count the ways: First, he held onto $71,000 he was supposed to pay to people attending a conference; then, he neglected to return another $25,000 in unused cash advances. Next, he used an undetermined amount of Institute money to support his other businesses. Afterward, he loaned over $100,000 of government money to friends and associates. Next, he overstated salaries by $23,000. Finally, this sterling citizen accepted, without comment, overpayments of $20,000 resulting from the Institute's inept accounting procedures.

The military can also be exceedingly generous with your tax dollars. For example, the Navy's Training Equipment Center in Orlando distinguished itself by paying $511 for a light bulb that cost 60 cents at the local store. Another Navy procurement officer, Mr. Generosity himself, paid $100 for aircraft simulator parts that cost exactly a nickel down at the hardware store—this is only a 199,900 percent markup. Astronomical, isn't it? But you haven't seen anything yet. Wait

3

until we get into the really big numbers.

In Mississippi, a supplier sold the Navy, at a price of $256, a gravity timer he had bought for only $11. That's a 2,227 percent markup. If this sounds like small stuff, remember than in 1984 the Department of Defense will spend about $22 billion to purchase spare parts.

But it's not just a matter of individuals abusing the government. The government itself abuses the government, which is another way of saying that the government abuses you. The government is so busy giving money away, appeasing special interest groups, finding short-term and inadequate solutions to major problems, and, in general, attempting to conceal the pervasiveness of its influence, that there are very few adequate systems to control Federal activities. Tens of billions of dollars are wasted every year because of inadequate controls. It is almost impossible to grasp the concept of even one single billion. For example, there are 3,600 seconds in an hour and 31,536,000 seconds in a year.

So one billion equals about thirty-two years of seconds— try counting seconds (boom, boom, boom . . .) for half of your life and see how you feel about a billion. And tens of billions are wasted each year because of inadequate controls. Ten billion is 3.2 *centuries* in seconds—someone who started counting ten billion seconds in 1667 would just be finished this year.

So taxpayers and voters, who legally "control" the government, have no practical way to do so. The abuses are endless. For example:

- The Health and Human Services Department has routinely paid out Social Security benefits to some 8,000 dead people, whose need for them is, well, doubtful.
- The Urban Mass Transportation Administration spent $10 million to buy new computers to keep track of the $25 billion it controls in active, ongoing grants. Despite the

4

new computers, the agency has been unable to close its accounting books since 1979. No account reconciliations have been done since 1977. The UMTA has no central ledger showing who owes what to whom. So even with the computers, the agency has to compute its financial data by hand.

- The Veterans Administration has a hospital construction staff of eight hundred employees. But the Hospital Corporation of America, a private company, does the same work with a staff of fifty. In part, because of the bureaucratic layering at the VA, it takes that agency seven years to finish a project, versus two years at HCA. Overhead costs at the VA are four times greater than at HCA and other private-sector companies.
- Most of the subsidized mortgage loans made by the government in 1982 went to people who could have bought homes without government help. The typical mortgage revenue bond buyer had an income between $20,000 and $40,000 a year. Some 53 percent were among the more affluent half of the families in their states, with several earning over $50,000 a year.

I have just spent the better part of two years as chairman of a commission looking into inefficiency and abuse (like these examples) in the Federal government. I am absolutely appalled at what we found. In searching out government inefficiency, we found literally tens of billions of dollars of immediate savings that could be made without cutting back a single needed program. All the government needs to do in most cases is to adopt commonsense business management practices that every company must use, from the corner drug store on up to General Motors, if it is to succeed. With the budget deficit in the news every day, I wonder why our findings haven't been splashed across the headlines; in fact, they've hardly been noticed so far.

5

Briefly, let me introduce myself. My name is J. Peter Grace. I am Chairman and Chief Executive Officer of W. R. Grace & Co., a New York–based corporation with $6.2 billion in sales, primarily in chemicals, natural resources, and consumer goods. We produce some two hundred different products, in plants all over the world. I've been Chief Executive Officer of Grace since 1945, and I've been involved in government in a number of voluntary efforts, most recently as a member of the National Productivity Advisory Committee.

In February of 1982, President Reagan asked me (I'm a registered Democrat, if that matters) to chair a Presidential commission to study the government. The idea was to have responsible, competent businessmen review the management of the Federal government. Some 160 of America's top business leaders agreed to join me in the effort, and they contributed over $76 million worth of money, manpower, and materials to the task. Not one cent of government money was expended for the project, an unprecedented contribution by the private sector.

The Deficit Emergency

Individual incidents, like those cited, have generally been reported by the media as amusing anecdotes, and have been regarded by the public as an unavoidable cost of our sprawling Federal bureaucracy. Well, we can no longer afford to be amused by inadequate and irresponsible management of our government, because our future is in jeopardy. We are facing a crisis that cannot be ignored, and our amusement must be replaced with outrage. Outrage that our political leaders have spent us to the point of bankruptcy and beyond. Put simply, the Federal deficit—estimated at $184 billion for 1984—is already alarmingly high, and guaranteed to increase uncontrollably in the future if nothing is done.

Now there are two ways to lower the deficit: raise taxes or

6

reduce spending. Raising taxes is comparatively easy, while reducing spending requires hard political decisions. The point of the examples of waste that you've just read is that we can cut spending, without savaging the poor, collapsing the construction industry, ruining the farmers, or causing any of the other disastrous results that proponents of Big Government cite as arguments against curtailed spending. All we have to do is cut out the waste and inefficiency!

This we simply must do, because, as taxes approach confiscatory levels, our incentives to work hard and make the economy grow will be eliminated.

It used to be that deficits came and went with the economic tides. In recessions we ran a deficit because more people were getting unemployment checks and fewer were paying taxes. Then when the economy turned up, the deficit shrank as unemployment disappeared and tax revenues went up. Now, in the mid-1980s, we are trapped with what economists call a "structural deficit"—one that keeps growing regardless of the swings of the economy.

How did this state of affairs come about? Basically, Congress loves to spend money. (Who doesn't? You can't blame them, but we simply can't afford their excesses.) Then too, our government is full of inefficiency. It is run with a profound disregard for sound business management. The Pentagon is spendthrift, with a firm conviction that massive waste is an unavoidable cost of military preparedness. The cost of government retirement and social payments is clearly out of control. The interest on the national debt alone currently runs over $100 billion annually. And now, Congress is waging a hot campaign to raise income taxes once again. Congress always wants to raise taxes to pay for a deficit, but new taxes are seldom applied to reducing the deficit; they're used to fund new programs or expand old ones. When was the last time Congress used your taxes to reduce the Federal debt?

It never occurs to many Congressmen that a deficit is defined as a simple excess of spending over revenues. If you make $50,000 a year but have expenses of $100,000, you have a deficit. Now the most practical way to solve it is to cut back those expenses. Sell that 1965 gas-guzzler you bought cheap on a whim, but which gets six miles to the gallon. No more impulsive, free-spending trips to Atlantic City for a while. And stash your Sears charge card in the back corner of a desk drawer until things clear up.

Any child can understand this, but try to explain it to a Congressman. Your most honorable legislative representative will gape at you bug-eyed, as if you've just called his parentage into question. "What? Cut the budget? Don't you know that's impossible? Do you want the children of America to go to bed hungry? Do you want defense contractors to lay off workers?"

Cutting the budget to eliminate inefficiencies has nothing to do with children going hungry or businesses going bust. In fact, we can cut the budget in such a way that the children get better fed and businesses make more profit, while the average family pays less in taxes. Sound impossible? All it takes is a concerted effort to run our national government as efficiently as American business is run. Is that such a shocking idea?

To Congress, apparently it is. Congress doesn't want to reduce spending, it wants to raise taxes. And why not, from their point of view? Spending is very important to Congressmen. After all, the way Congressmen get votes and guarantee loyalties back in the home district is by "bringing home the bacon," whether the projects thus supported are worthwhile or not. A fancy new highway here, a military base there, a new dam in the middle of nowhere—this is the stuff of long-term incumbency; it is also how some Congressmen hope to get themselves immortalized, with their names carved in stone above the portals of some imposing Federally financed boondoggle. So when you speak of not raising taxes or, God forbid, even cutting them, you're threatening the mother lode

8

of Congressional patronage, and all but the most rare and eccentric of Congressmen will wail and fight against such a radical proposal like a cross, sleepy baby holding onto her Cabbage Patch doll. Cut spending? Perish the thought.

If you think the current and projected tax rates are already bad and counterproductive, you haven't seen anything yet. The fiscal 1983 deficit was $195 billion, and the only thing our best forecasters can see in the long term is disastrously higher deficits. Data Resources, Inc., perhaps the most respected economic forecasting firm in the country, predicts that if current policies are continued, by the year 2000, just sixteen years away, the Federal deficit will equal an astounding $2 trillion, ten times the 1983 deficit. That's not the total debt of the Federal government, it's just the yearly gap between spending and receipts. Two trillion dollars! If you divide that figure by the population of America, it comes out to roughly $8,500 per person in that year alone. How are you going to pay off your $8,500? This amount, of course, is above and beyond your tax bill. And it doesn't include your share of the national debt, which will total $13 trillion in that year, or an average of $169,000 per current taxpayer.

A forecast sixteen years out into the future is always an educated guess, but in this case, unhappily, the forecast looks conservative. There's simply nothing that will make the deficit go away, unless we resolve the now built-in spending trend. If we elect a free-spending President or two, the figure could balloon even further. Economic prosperity wouldn't make much of a dent in the deficit figure as it has in the past.

Deep Truths of the Pocketbook

If appeals to our nation's future productivity and prosperity don't move you, then take a look at how much the deficit is already costing you. It used to be, back in the good old days of 1971, that a family of four making $16,000 a year (not bad money in 1971), paid 19 percent of its income in the form of taxes. By 1981, the amount of income going to pay taxes for a comparable family of four had increased to 30 percent. That's a big bite out of the family budget. In fact, taxes now make up the biggest single household budget item, whereas in 1971, housing and food, individually, accounted for larger shares of the family budget.

Between 1971 and 1981 the share of income that taxes took from this family rose 56 percent. This occurred while the share that food and housing took decreased 3.5 percent and 11.6 percent, respectively. You might have heard on television that medical costs are the main culprit in the family budget squeeze, but, between 1971 and 1981, medical costs rose from 4 percent to 5.1 percent of the family's budget—a significant increase, but hardly a major item of expense compared to the 30 percent of the family's budget taken by taxes.

So today, the median-income family, which earned $24,100 in 1983, pays $2,218 a year in Federal income taxes, up from $9 in 1948. In 1948, the median-income family earned $3,187 annually; in other words, taxes have increased 32.4 times faster than income for this family. And that's while the deficit went from a surplus of $12 billion in 1948 to a deficit of $195 billion in 1983. The median-income family would have to pay $3,833 in Federal taxes—73 percent more than it currently pays—just to balance the budget, let alone create a surplus.

Between 1965 and 1983, the Federal government upped its take of your personal income through taxes from $49 billion to $289 billion, almost a sixfold increase. But it seems that isn't enough. Congress wants more and more of your income, and still the deficit grows larger. And they'll get it, sooner or later, if we don't cut the budget as outlined in these chapters. If you hope to hold onto the money you make in the future, we have to stop the government's spending madness.

One good indicator of the self-defeating nature of our high income taxes is the "underground economy." In recent years it has swelled to an estimated $100 billion a year in uncollected taxes, triple the estimated amount in 1973. Some people live almost totally in this underground economy, working "off the books" for tax-free cash, and buying for cash in unrecorded tax-free transactions at a discount.

A few pundits argue that Americans are scandalously undertaxed compared to the citizens of other nations, in relation to the amount of government we demand. How are we undertaxed compared with other nations? First, if you look at other nations, many have tax systems that provide much greater work incentives than ours. For example, the U.S. relies about one-half as much on consumption taxes as do France and Germany. Consumption taxes encourage productiveness and saving; and the German savings rate is 2.3 times higher than ours. But beyond the matter of how confiscatory our taxes are, even if we demand big government, our taxes aren't paying for it. All of our personal income taxes are not enough to pay for the Federal share of income transfer programs, and interest on the national debt.

So why not just tax the rich, as some political candidates loudly demand? Okay, if it makes us feel good. And if we don't mind our wealthy investors parking their money overseas, which they surely will. And if we don't mind our star producers quitting and joining the underground economy. But as for raising money, if we take all income above $75,000 a year that isn't already taxed, take it all, leave no one anything above $75,000, we'd raise the sum of $17 billion, enough to run the government for about ten days.

The fact is that 90 percent of all our taxable income is accounted for by income brackets of $35,000 a year or less. That's where the money is. At the level of $75,000 and above, there just isn't that much revenue available.

I am not saying that taxpayers with taxable incomes of $35,000 and below account for 90 percent of taxable income—they account for something like 75 percent according to IRS data. I am saying that tax *brackets* $35,000 and below account for 90 percent of taxable income, i.e., counting the fraction of *everyone's* taxable income that flows through these brackets, we arrive at the 90 percent figure. On this basis, for example, 50 percent of the taxable income of someone earning $70,000 would be considered as having "flowed-through" brackets $35,000 and below.

So when you hear pleas to reduce the deficit by raising taxes, remember it has to come out of the hides of median-income families, whose tax bills have already increased 246 times since 1948 (though their incomes went up only 7.6 times during the period). I emphasize it again—lower and middle-income Americans are already overtaxed. But if we don't reduce Federal spending, absurdly higher taxes are just what we'll get—no matter who's President. There'll be no alternative.

On the Backs of Our Children

The year 2000 isn't as far away as it sounds. Time does have a way of creeping up on one. Only sixteen years ago, Lyndon Johnson was in his last term of office and Richard Nixon was being elected, which doesn't seem that long ago. Now by the year 2000 you may be retired in your present modest or not-so-modest home or in a Cocoa Beach condo. But what about your children? Is this the legacy you wish to offer them? Let's look at just what legacy I'm talking about—a $2 trillion annual deficit despite a massive increase in our total personal income taxes. Right now Federal, state, and local taxes take more than a third of your hard-earned income. How will you or your kids feel when everyone is forced to give up double that amount to taxes?

But this is only the beginning of your children's troubles. For soon the American population will include such a large percentage of older citizens that a relatively small number of active workers will be paying Social Security for a huge number of retirees. In 1945, there were 42 Social Security contributors per beneficiary. There were 16.5 by 1950. By 1980, there were 3.3. In the year 2015, it is estimated that there will only be 2.8. The median age is already near 30, and, with more people living longer, the Social Security burden a few years hence will be heavy indeed. The good news is that people are living longer; the bad news is that Social Security may not be able to make that continue to be good news. Already there is a $1.7 trillion unfunded liability in the Social Security system. That means that Social Security taxes in the future will have to be substantially higher (and you thought they were bad enough already!), since they have increased for the median-income American family from $30 a year in the late 1940s to more than $1,600 today.

I don't know about you, but it makes me see red. Oceans of red ink from current spending and from future liabilities—such as Social Security—for which not enough money is being put away. Liabilities that will bankrupt our children and limit their freedom. It is almost obscene to see middle-income Americans handing over one-third of their incomes to pay Federal, state, and local taxes—taxes that are paid in large part to support Congress's addiction to spending. That's what we call confiscatory taxation. Remember, from history class, the Boston Tea Party? The colonials' refusal to pay confiscatory British taxes was instrumental in causing us to break away from the mother country. They protested "Taxation without Representation." Well, now we have taxation with representation, except that it's the special interests who are represented, organized groups, who yearn for Congress to spend money on their pet projects and schemes. Ill-conceived spending that ignores the consequences for the American economy.

And if you think that somehow by the year 2000 everyone will be making a lot more money because the economy will be better, the reverse is far more likely to be true. With the deficit at $2 trillion, we'll live in a state of more or less permanent stagflation—and with many of our freedoms lost or severely curtailed. A deficit that big will virtually halt business spending for plant and equipment—the kind of spending that creates new jobs. (On the other hand, if the recommendations sketched in this book are put into effect, we'll reduce the deficit to $37 billion by 2000 and create two million more jobs.) Doing nothing, on the other hand, will feed a nagging inflation of something close to 10 percent a year. This is our gift to future generations. I'm sure they'll be most appreciative. They'll probably look back to the low inflation and relative prosperity of 1983 and 1984 with nostalgia and anger—if we do nothing today to solve the deficit problem while it is still solvable.

While the huge deficits are bad news, the government is, in fact, substantially understating the real deficit by a bewildering assortment of incomprehensible accounting procedures. If the government were required to meet the same regulations as business, it would need to set aside money each year to pay off future obligations. But the government doesn't have to, and so it doesn't. Instead it is pushing costs into the future. How much? Almost a $3-trillion liability for past services under the Social Security and government pension systems and more than $1 billion in public debt. These amounts will mushroom as the American population grows older, as it is quickly doing. Now if you were to count the amounts of money needed to cover all these retirement obligations, you come out with a fiscal 1983 budget deficit that is not $195 billion but almost double that at $382 billion. And the $2-trillion deficit expected in the year 2000 becomes $3.8 trillion. Numbers this huge are beyond our comprehension. So once again, for perspective, it takes more than 1,200 *centuries* of seconds to equal 3.8 trillion, over sixty times the period from the birth of Christ.

14

How Long Will the Arabs Pump Money into the U.S.?

If the current budget deficit is so bad, why isn't the economy being negatively affected? One reason is simply that foreign money has been doing an excellent job of "covering" the deficit. We can't expect this to go on indefinitely. That foreign money isn't exactly patriotic. It will pull out at the first hint of an excuse. We are becoming increasingly dependent on foreign governments whose interests are often 180 degrees away from ours. They will not hesitate to use their economic bargaining chips for leverage when it suits their purposes.

Overseas, the frequent complaint is that the dollar is too strong (and when the dollar is weak, the complaint is that the dollar is too weak). It's fashionable to use the dollar as an easy excuse for all their economic ills. People around the world often love America for its wealth, but detest Americans for being well-off. They drink our Coca-Cola, eat our Big Macs, watch our movies, and their kids listen to Michael Jackson, but that doesn't mean they want the same things we want or buy our vision of the world.

The current strong dollar is partly a result of our large deficits. When we have a large deficit—that is, a big excess of expenses over receipts—the government has to pay for the difference somehow—by raising taxes, printing money, or borrowing. Neither raising taxes nor printing money provides cash as quickly as borrowing, so the Treasury goes into the credit markets and borrows the cash to keep things running. It does this by selling Treasury bonds. These are beautifully engraved pieces of paper promising that if you give the Treasury, say, $1,000 today, then in six months or a year, or whatever the term may be, it will return to you that $1,000, plus a percentage profit equal to the interest rate on the bond (which is taxable to you, of course).

15

Now when the Treasury goes into the credit markets to borrow, it goes into the credit markets in a big way. It may go in on a given day to borrow $10 billion at a time. Even in these days of a $3.3-trillion U.S. economy, $10 billion is still a great deal of money. The Treasury has to compete with other borrowers for available funds. So in order to sell its bonds, the Treasury offers interest rates that are higher relative to risk than those offered by competing borrowers. The Treasury thus sells off its bonds and meets its cash requirements.

But a curious thing also happens. All other interest rates soon follow the Treasury bonds' lead. In financial jargon, other interest rates are "pegged" to the Treasury borrowing rate. Why? Because Treasury bonds are the safest form of investment. They are backed up by the vast wealth of the American economy. They are also backed by the government's ability to print the money it needs.

Some of the most avid buyers of Treasury bonds are rich foreign investors, who view U.S. Government securities as safer investments than the securities of their own governments. In recent years, the Arabs have been the most prominent of these overseas investors. But there are many wealthy Europeans, Asians, and Latin Americans who love to purchase U.S. Treasury bills, because they see them as the safest investments in the world, safer by far than anything available, anywhere else in the world. They might criticize our country, but they trust us with their gold.

Which is fortunate for us. Because with our deficit so large, that foreign investment in Treasury bonds is a major contributing factor to maintaining our economic stability. If that overseas investment wasn't available, it would be difficult to finance the Federal budget without disrupting the economy. In 1983, foreigners held $160.2 billion, or 14 percent, of the total debt held by the public, versus only 5 percent in 1970. At year-end 1982, foreign investment in U.S. businesses amounted to an additional $121.9 billion, further easing the pressure for capital that would otherwise have to be met by the U.S. credit market.

Senior monetary officials are concerned about this situation and recognize that it isn't safe for us to be so dependent on foreign money. The foreign money that is here today can just as easily leave tomorrow. It's free-floating money, searching only for the safest and most lucrative resting-place. Further, the Arab nations are relatively short of cash in comparison to the amounts that were available at OPEC's peak. Now that oil seems plentiful and we're using less of it, less cash is being generated by the oil-exporting countries. Many of these countries have committed themselves to huge projects in their own countries that have to be completed. The continued availability of foreign investment is by no means a certainty.

The high interest rates keeping that foreign money here also stifle business investment and spending, which are heavily financed by borrowing. Investment is the key to America's future. It is needed to fund research and development, build modern factories, and enter into new industries—without which we'll lose our rank as the foremost world economy. Already, we are hard-pressed to compete in automobiles and steel. America is now behind Japan in robotics. And we are being challenged in such areas as computers, where we once led indisputably.

Nor are those high rates much help if you want to buy a house or car. Normally, high interest rates lead to recession. Low rates are really what get the economy off and going. And in fact, the deficit-driven interest rates have forced the median-income American family to pay 44 percent of its income to finance the purchase of its home, up from half that amount in 1970. Today, the monthly carrying charges for a house run to $875, five times the amount paid in 1970. Pity the young marrieds of today!

With the outsized deficit, the only way we can have low

17

interest rates is by making a pact with the Devil, who appears in the guise of inflation. The Federal government, specifically the Federal Reserve Board, is fully capable of forcing down interest rates temporarily. It can do this by cranking up the printing presses and flooding the economy with cash. Interest rates will drop as money becomes more available, and soon you'll feel more prosperous. But the new prosperity will be a sham, because inflation will return in spades and your money will become relatively worthless. We could even end up like Germany after the First World War, where you had to bring a wheelbarrow of cash to the local rathskeller if you wanted a glass of draft beer.

Remember those days of the late 1960s when the Fed pumped money into the economy to finance the Vietnam War? President Lyndon Johnson, you may recall, had refused to propose a tax increase to pay for guns and butter. "All of us know that we are now in the fifty-second month of the prosperity that's been unequaled in this nation, and I see no reason for declaring a national emergency," said he. So the government had to sell Treasury bonds to pay for the war, and in order to mitigate the rise in interest rates, the Fed poured money into the economy. Result? The inflation of the early 1970s and the subsequent deep recession of 1975.

Respect Must Be Earned

Let us return for a moment to the matter of the dishpan hands, the irreconcilable account books, and the rest. Yes, it's costing us plenty, and this kind of waste is morally repugnant. It isn't just that this is wrong. Of course it is that. But here is our Federal government, the maker and upholder of our laws, the supposed expression of our collective will, making a mockery of us. We are a nation that has always valued personal liberty and resisted centralized authority. We

18

want exemplary figures in charge of things. We need ideals. We expect our leaders to be better than average, morally upright, bigger than life.

Lately some public figures complain that Americans are getting cynical. Not long ago, a candidate for President accused Americans of becoming "Europeanized" in their disrespect of the tax laws. Well, Americans, in fact, will respect the government in proportion to its respectability. The kind of gross waste and abuse that exists in our government must be swept away before the government can command respect. Indeed, it is immoral to ask Americans to pay yet higher tax burdens before the government has made a full commitment to the elimination of waste and inefficiency in its operations.

Why Aren't We Marching on Capitol Hill?

Most of us are aware in some vague way that there's a problem with government spending. It is certainly clear by the red ink of our bankbooks that taxes have become more burdensome, even as government services decline. Just look at our deteriorating dams, bridges, and highways. Then we're told our tax money is needed to pay for social programs, but all the money we spend doesn't seem to materially change the amount of poverty. We know we need a strong defense, but why pay billions more than necessary for all manner of items from screws to military bases?

In this vague perception, the people are still several steps ahead of their leaders. A large part of the political process in America today is simply the arduous task of educating our leaders as to what's going on in the country and as to what the people think about it. We have in our country the fastest, most sophisticated systems of communications known to man. Yet despite all the daily polls, newspaper stories, magazine articles, books, television and radio reports, on-line computer information, electronic mail, the U.S. Postal Service, and even the telephone, Washington remains shrouded in a dense fog of unreality.

Washington Fever is a dangerous thing, too. In many a case, a Congressman loses perspective on why he was elected and what his responsibilities are. There's little time for the complexities of government. There are meetings with special interest groups and money to be raised to finance the next election.

But, back down to earth, the taxi driver and the housewife wonder why it is that they can't get away with spending more than they earn when the government is able to. And they are aware that there is waste in the government. They might have read one of those occasional news stories highlighting an instance of government extravagance. They might have seen television accounts or read newspaper articles on Congressional junkets.

So why aren't we marching on Capitol Hill? Oh, there are lots of reasons. First, the sort of people who are most likely to worry about the deficit and the attendant runaway taxation are not the sort of people who usually march in the streets. Mostly they are too busy earning a living to take up banners of protest. But even more likely, marching in the streets is not to their taste. It is, well, unseemly for anyone above college age.

Second, the whole deficit issue, as filtered through the media, is many-sided and unclear. Yes, one feels, there is tremendous waste in government. But one then also sees on television that whosoever wants to cut the budget is hardhearted, bent on making poor people suffer. Maybe Washington knows what it's doing, and the people complaining about the budget are confused or malicious. It seems very complicated. However, the deficit is only a symptom of the real problem— Federal spending—and, if the facts are known, the issue becomes quite clear.

What the Nightly News Forgot to Mention

The media don't help. Television news, pervasive as it is, could do a lot more. Now television reporters are nice people. They are generally bright, decently educated, and sophisticated. But as a group, they tend to think too much alike. Actually, many so-called television journalists aren't journalists at all, in any meaningful sense of the word. They're performers.

These high-powered TV celebrities tend to adhere to a set of values that makes them veritable cheerleaders for Big Government. If there are poor people in America, it's because the government hasn't spent enough money on poverty programs. If cars are unsafe, it's because the government hasn't come down hard enough on the "big businessmen" who manufacture cars. They assume that if there's a problem, what we need is more government, not less, to solve it. In an age when most people get their daily news from television, it is hard to overestimate the mischief of this thinking.

The network news will, from time to time, report an amusing example of government waste. But our herd of television journalists has little room in their thinking for the idea that Big Government can be, in fact usually is, extremely inefficient, scandalously so. Thus, if there are people starving on the streets, they tend not to entertain the possibility that it is because government poverty programs are so ill-managed that the money isn't going where it's needed. (That, indeed, is the case, as we will see.)

A whole generation of American journalists and opinion leaders has been greatly influenced by Watergate, in which the press played virtuous hero, uncovering the seamy underside of the Federal government. With that sort of precedent, you'd think that journalists would be crawling through every agency in Washington, seeking out waste and fraud, hoping to win fame and fortune in another Watergate-style coup. Isn't it

odd that none of this occurs? Isn't it strange that our journalists, who are so anxious to reveal instances in which government apparently has not spent enough, are so utterly un-
interested in discovering where it has spent too much? Isn't it
curious that the press finds even the most outrageous examples of government waste and abuse hardly worth any mention at all?

I believe that the television medium instills in viewers a
sense of powerlessness. First, we are conditioned by television
to sit by watching passively as great events pass on our little
screens, made smaller than life. We are disconnected from
these events in any real sense. They are not a part of us, and
they seem to happen without any participation on our part.
It's as if we don't really matter. The only people who matter
are the ones underneath the hot lights. I suspect that in the
days when we depended on newspapers, magazines, and
books for our information, we had a more intimate sense of
the reality of events. Reading, or even listening to the radio, is
a much more intellectual activity than staring at a television
screen. When we read or listen to the radio, our minds and
imaginations are actively involved. Well, we can't go back to
the old technologies. But we can recognize the effects of the
new ones, and adjust to them as much as is possible.

Maybe there is also a very basic difficulty here, one that
affects journalists as much as it does the public. The numbers
are so large, the inefficiencies so vast! If we speak of the Pentagon wasting $5 billion a year on this or that item, can any-
one conceive of so huge an amount of money in any realistic
sense? I have a great deal of trouble doing so. A billion dollars
is one thousand million dollars. If you had a billion, you could
spend $100,000 a day, every day, and you could keep on doing
this for 27 years—though I imagine that well before then
you'd get bored with all your money. Numbers in the billions
generally become meaningless, because they are beyond ordinary comprehension. Now we are talking about even larger

amounts, trillions of dollars. Remember, a trillion equals 317 centuries of seconds. As the late Senator Everett Dirksen of Illinois said, "A billion here, a billion there, pretty soon we're talking about real money." Well, what it actually adds up to is Unreal Money.

A Crusade against Government Waste

In any case, what can one do to influence such gigantic problems involving so many thousands of millions of dollars? Write a complaining letter to the Pentagon? You can imagine that such a letter might eventually reach some junior-level assistant to an assistant to an assistant, who six months later might reply by sending you a form letter whose content is entirely unrelated to the subject of your letter, and which also is mailed to you in an incorrectly addressed envelope.

Not very encouraging. And that is a great shame, because the only way we'll get government running right, running smoothly and efficiently at minimum cost, is by public pressure from the grass roots level. As long as you don't care, or as long as the government, especially Congress, thinks you don't care, nothing will be done. It is my great hope that by the time you finish this book, you'll want to do something, and you will actually take a bit of time and do it. We, as members of the public, are not powerless. Our voices, and our votes, do count. All we have to do is to make them heard in the most effective ways. It is our duty as citizens to do so, if not for ourselves, then for our children.

Toward the end of this book, I'll talk about some concrete things you might do to exert pressure in Washington, to cure this mess. Your help is sorely needed. In fact, the whole effort to eliminate the deficit and make the government more efficient ultimately depends on you. As for myself, I'm doing everything I can think of to help.

23

What we need is a crusade—a crusade of the people—to force Congress to clean up government waste and abuse, so our government will work as efficiently as it's supposed to, getting services out to those who need them, taking proper care of the national defense, the administration of justice, and the other things that government can do better than private enterprise, and doing it without costing our citizens ever higher, ever more confiscatory taxes. We can do it, if you help.

Chapter 2

Before the Deficit

The Federal budget deficit didn't develop in a vacuum, and it didn't suddenly start like spontaneous combustion. The deficit has long historical roots that must be understood if we are to know what to do. There have been a number of trends over the last five decades that have contributed toward its creation.

First, we mistakenly came to believe, after the tragedy of the Great Depression, that for solving economic problems bigger government is better and a lot more trustworthy and effective than private initiatives. This view found support particularly among Keynesian economists, who saw the purse strings of government as a means of regulating the economy. Next, in the sixties we fundamentally altered our notion of social justice. In the seventies, after Vietnam, we wallowed in weakness. Post-Watergate, Congress became even more a collection of selfish special interests. In our collective anxiety, we let government grow ever bigger. Now, will we wake up before it is too late?

Men in Boxcars

Remember those grainy old black-and-white newsreel films of the Great Depression? There were sad-faced men selling apples and pencils on the sidewalk. Ragged, unshaven men were crowded in freight cars, headed to undetermined places, searching for work. There were scenes of other, faintly smiling men digging ditches and planting saplings for the Civilian Conservation Corps.

And there was President Franklin D. Roosevelt, with his patrician smile, cigarette in a long holder, riding in his open-top car, waving to the crowds. Seated before one of those primitive microphones of the day, he was depicted delivering a "fireside chat." His government would get the nation out of this mess, get it back working again, he promised. The Civilian Conservation Corps, the Works Progress Administration, and a host of grab-bag New Deal agencies would create employment where there was none, to get money back into the people's pockets, and to restore a measure of dignity to those thousands who had been humiliated by the Depression's hardships.

The nation was in sore need of a new deal. Capitalism, it seemed, had failed disastrously. The free and untrammeled pursuit of profit had only led to unprecedented loss, bankruptcy, even starvation, it appeared. If the business of America was business, then America had gone bust.

Quite naturally, the horrible experience of the Great Depression embittered a great many men toward capitalism. The anger began with men who originally had held capitalism in high esteem, and who were, often as not, capitalists themselves. Men like Henry Luce, the founder of *Time* magazine, were fed up and resentful of the seeming excesses of business. His anger soon was reflected in the columns of his magazines. Even *Fortune*, which he had established on the eve of the Depression specifically to celebrate American capitalism, was to become for years a severe critic of business.

The anger reached its ultimate expression in the influential circle of New York intellectuals, many of whom turned to Marxism. Their influence lasted well into the 1950s, when news of Stalin's mass murders in Russia made Marxism less fashionable. At some distance from the Marxist extremists stood a vast majority of Roosevelt Democrats, determined that never again would another depression be allowed to ravage the nation.

The working hypothesis of Franklin Roosevelt's New Deal was that Big Government would do what private business had so ignominiously failed to do: Government would not only provide jobs, it would also ensure old people's retirement with a new program called Social Security, and it would give money to the unemployed. Government would become the overseer of the nation's economic welfare. Thus the American welfare state was born. And this welfare state has extended its guiding hand into the affairs of American business, regulating every aspect that might impinge on the public well-being. Never again, it was thought, would business be given carte blanche to ruin the nation in the name of all-powerful profits.

Enter Lord Keynes, Stage Left

In response to the Great Depression, John Maynard Keynes, a British economist, developed a theory to both explain what had happened and to provide a way out. Keynes theorized that the capitalist economy did not always automatically bring supply and demand into balance when left to its own devices, as had been thought since Adam Smith. Rather, said Keynes, the economy might "stabilize" at some unacceptable level of unemployment. And traditional remedies, such as lower interest rates—which would encourage a recovery—could not work if prices were falling. Government, Keynes said, could cure this by spending money—even borrowed money—to restart the economy. Even hiring the unemployed just to dig useless ditches would solve things by putting money into people's hands, by "priming the pump." After all, Keynes stated, in good times the money would be repaid from government surpluses.

So it was this British economist who gave theoretical legitimacy to the notion that government budget deficits, in times

27

of recession or depression, are good things. Indeed, Keynes preached that any government that refused to run a deficit in times of recession was hardhearted and shortsighted.

I have oversimplified the Keynesian phenomenon, but it's hard to overemphasize the intellectual excitement Keynes's new theory created in the thirties and forties. This new theory was couched in elegant, often obscure technical terms. It made a whole generation of young economists feel like a band of Einsteins at the brink of important new discoveries. Keynes offered a new and seemingly revolutionary paradigm to replace the conventional economic wisdom. At the great universities, Keynesianism breathed fresh excitement into the profession.

Also, most conveniently, it gave new status to economists within the government. Keynesian theory taught that economists, in Washington or London, could "fine-tune" the economy to provide permanent full employment through the careful management of deficit spending. If it were only true, Keynesian economics would mean a permanent end to recessions and depressions.

Of course, it didn't happen that way. While "priming the pump" helped—and provided work and food for millions who might otherwise have gone hungry—it was the onset of the Second World War that pulled our economy out of the Great Depression. In 1939, after six years of boondoggling, for example, the unemployment rate still averaged 17.2 percent versus 3.2 percent in 1929. The massive spending on war material, the rapid mobilization to a wartime economy, set the nation humming with industry. Auto assembly lines were converted overnight into tank assembly lines. Textile mills turned out olive drab cloth for uniforms. Women for the first time were given widespread employment, simply because a lot of men were off to fight in the war, and our factories were working overtime to meet the needs of the Allies.

Well then, Keynes was right, wasn't he? Government

spending got us out of the Depression. Yes, in a vulgar sense. Massive government spending, or any other kind of massive spending, will obviously make an economy boom. But that doesn't tell us anything very useful. World war is not exactly a viable economic policy, except in a madman's vision.

The wartime economy transformed America from a quiet, somewhat isolated, inward-looking country into the greatest superpower of the twentieth century. Private industry proved in spades that it could meet any challenge in terms of quantities of industrial output such as autos and airplanes, and also innovate in the high-tech areas of computers, nuclear energy, and the like.

In a finer sense, Keynes was also right—it is appropriate for a government to spend money it doesn't have in bad times, thus creating deficits, which are balanced by surpluses created in good times. Today we call this balancing the budget over the business cycle. Unfortunately, as we have seen during fifteen years of continual deficits, it is a good deal easier to open the government spending spigot than it is to turn it off. And every nickel of deficit spending—even when we are "finetuning" a healthy economy with more spending—is done in the name of "Keynesianism," even though it may be the opposite of what Keynes himself would have recommended.

Welcome to—the Affluent Society

Then came the boom. At war's end, America was born anew—this time bigger and better than ever. The sun shone bright in the warm spring of peacetime. The relieved nation went on a postwar spending spree. There was a rush by veterans to buy homes; refrigerators and washing machines disappeared from the stores. Back at home, our soldiers were honored victors. America was at the height of her powers, politically, economically, and—with sole possession of The Bomb—militarily.

29

We can see, upon reflection, that our values and fundamental assumptions were evolving from the long night of the
Depression, though the bad memory never left our collective
conscious; in fact, that memory made security the most
sought-after postwar virtue. At war's end, we were a calm,
secure, homogeneous nation, unified by our victory and our
newfound affluence. America was the finest country, and its
government was sound. Good jobs were available, waiting for
men to fill them: Those who hadn't been able to afford a
college education could now go almost for free, thanks to
veterans' benefits. Then they could sign on with a prospering
large corporation and work their way up to the top. Back then,
there was plenty of room at the top, in fact a crying need for
middle- and upper-level managers. Affording a suburban
colonial or ranch-style home was made relatively easy by low-
interest loans for veterans. Soon a station wagon would grace
the curving black-top driveway, and before long a tiny wood-
encased television screen would make its appearance in the
den. Median-family income soared by 64 percent between
1947 and 1957, to $4,966.

Washington was still a quiet Southern city in the 1950s.
The pace was as languid as the hot summer air. Nobody much
cared if President Eisenhower snoozed at his desk, or if Congress took long vacations. The nation seemed to more or less
run itself. The Federal budget stayed mostly in surplus,
though there was a small $7-billion deficit in the mild reces-
sion year of 1953. Inflation "raged" at 2 percent to 3 percent a
year, with unemployment seldom above 5 percent per year.

America's Mid-life Crisis

Money, of course, doesn't bring happiness, and often is
the root of much unhappiness. So it was that the affluence of
the 1950s turned into the uproarious 1960s, when it was generally thought that the prosperity of American society could

be assumed as a given, and forgotten about. In the 1960s, it would be time to perfect our society. Upon Eisenhower's retirement in 1960, the Utopian intellectuals and ideologues who had suffered in grudging silence under Ike found a perfect ally in John F. Kennedy.

Young, handsome, witty, every bit as patrician as Roosevelt had been and properly respectful of academics, Kennedy was a liberal intellectual's dream come true. Never mind that JFK was actually rather right-wing when it came to national defense (his speeches make later Republican Presidents sound like quivering wimps by comparison). Never mind that initially Kennedy opposed desegregation efforts. And never mind, in retrospect, that it was Kennedy who put us into Vietnam.

Here was where our values really seemed, in the reflective glare of the media, to change drastically. The frugal, security-conscious, deeply conservative, Depression-scarred values of the 1950s would now be shoved aside, we were told, to make way for bolder new visions of American Utopia. The agent of that utopia would be the Federal government, guided by the wisdom of Keynesian intellectuals no longer bound by the humdrum constraints of merely making a living—constraints that did, unfortunately, concern the millions of ordinary Americans who quietly went about their daily toils outside the gates of the ivory tower.

All among us, except for the very young, recall the tumult that followed in the 1960s: We recall it with varying mixtures of revulsion, nostalgia, and perhaps some lingering puzzlement. What a different world it had become! A kaleidoscopic jumble of riots, marches, screams and protests, assassinations, wild talk of revolution. Music turned hard and electronic, hair got long, and the old values became objects of amusement. You may not be surprised to learn that sociologists later found between 1957 and 1972 a marked downturn in the number of those who described their lives as "very

31

happy." But the number began to climb upward again in the late 1970s.

The New Right to Welfare

The year 1964 wasn't a signal year in terms of oppression or acid rock or women's liberation, but it did mark a turning point in social thinking, which has had a profound effect on government spending. Social scientists now tend to agree that around 1964 our leaders decided that the quest for equal opportunity, begun in earnest during the civil rights protests, was not sufficient. Instead of equality of opportunity, now we would pursue equality of results. A citizen now had more than the right to compete; he had the right to win.

The consequences of this shift in social thinking were immense. Instead of concentrating on making sure that minorities received the best possible training and preparation so they could take their place in society as equals alongside the majority, now the idea was that each American had a right—an "entitlement"—to welfare.

At the most practical level, government social workers strove to offer welfare, food stamps, housing subsidies, and the rest, to all comers. Not just to all comers: Since the middle 1970s, government social workers have made it a practice to literally go out banging on doors to sign people up for food stamps. They do this on the theory that many people are ignorant of food stamps, and must be actively recruited into the program. Then, of course, one can't overlook the fact that the more recipients a local food stamp office recruits, the bigger the local food stamp office budget will become, and the greater the power that will accrue to the bureaucrat in charge. Such is the nature of government bureaucracy.

Well, of course, this shift to equality of results led to a huge increase in social welfare spending during the 1970s. What has been the result? The level of poverty, unfortunately, has stayed the same regardless of these increased expenditures. Federal spending for "means-tested" antipoverty programs (those offering benefits according to one's lack of "means") went from $12.6 billion in 1959 to $78.8 billion in 1983, in real terms—up 6.3 times. Yet the poverty level, which initially declined from 22 percent in 1960 to 11 percent in 1973, began to increase since the mid-seventies to 15 percent of the population in 1982.

What is one to conclude? The work we did on the government budget for President Reagan did not involve assumptions about government policy, other than the assumption that it would not change. I therefore have no interest here in suggesting one welfare policy or another. But facts are facts, and these facts do help explain how budget deficits have become a way of life—and a reckless one—for American society. Let's at least know what we're talking about.

To Be Right-wing, or to Be Right?

The idea of cutting government spending itself is unfortunately associated with those disparagingly labeled as right-wing. The reasoning generally goes like this: People who dare to entertain the faintest notions of cutting government spending are obviously mean, hardhearted, compassionless people. Ergo, those who want to cut government spending are right-wingers.

The essence of this argument is in the word "compassion." What does it really mean?

Is it "compassion" for the Federal government to spend twice as much, per bed, as the private sector in constructing hospitals, or four times as much for nursing homes? Do the people who legislate these kinds of public expenditures ever think about the greater number of beds and better service

33

that could be provided if this sort of profligacy were eliminated? In other words, does one have to be mindless to be also "compassionate"?

Is it "compassion" that motivates our elected representatives to keep open hundreds of unneeded military bases? Think of the compassion that could be shown if billions of dollars spent in this way were targeted to where our national security would be strengthened.

Is it "compassion" that moves our Congress to provide free Coast Guard towing services for rich yacht owners?

Is it compassionate for a government agency managing public buildings to employ seventeen times as many people and spend fourteen times as much money as a private sector firm with comparable responsibilities?

Is it "compassion" that causes Congress to grant Civil Service and military personnel pension benefits from three to six times as generous as those of their private-sector counterparts?

I could go on like this, but you get the point. "Compassion" has become a phony, debased word in the mouths of politicians.

And to consider any talk of cutting the budget as some species of extreme right-wing anathema is the sort of Newspeak to make George Orwell blanch. That kind of slander is a handy political tool for the many politicos who are hungry for your tax dollars, and for the journalists who serve as their camp followers. But we can't let them get away with this distortion. To advocate an efficient, sound, honest government is neither left-wing nor right-wing. It is just plain right.

Chapter 3

The Failed Culture

Fingers in the Pudding

As we continued our analysis of government operations, we kept running into a basic obstruction to improving operating efficiency: We found that Congress interferes constantly with the day-to-day management of Federal agencies and departments, contrary to all the rules of good management. In private business, we know that the more a board of directors or top-level management is involved with day-to-day decisions, the less effective the operating management becomes. This is especially true over the long haul when an operating management—shackled by these unwanted attentions—becomes unable to react to the changes in its marketplace environment. When you have a board of directors, or a Congress, breathing down your neck, you tend not to do anything that will rock the boat.

Good management—simplified—works like this: You tell those who execute programs what to accomplish, not how to do the job. You set goals. You give management the tools and the authority to accomplish the job. You also give them the flexibility to use their resources as they best see fit. As a board, you monitor this management to see if it's accomplishing the stated mission and you measure results. But you don't saddle management with an outside presence that tells it how to do its job, and you don't constantly meddle in even the smallest details of management operations. And yet, Congress *is* meddling (it's called micromanagement) to the great detriment of the government's efficiency.

I recognize that the complexities of the checks and balances system in the U.S. Government make the analogy between private sector and public sector practices less than a perfect one. Still, time-tested management principles do have relevance to the relationship between Congress, which makes the laws, and the Executive Branch, which carries them out.

While the Survey certainly has no competence or desire to argue constitutional issues, still it appeared to us as professional executives and managers that there is a significant dollar cost to Congressional encroachment in the management of federal agencies.

Here are a few examples:

Among the four thousand U.S. military installations, few would argue that all are efficient or necessary. But of the seventeen military installations formally slated by the Department of Defense for closing since 1977, only three have actually been shut down. One military base was set for closing in 1964, 1970, 1978, and 1979. In 1981, the Defense Department finally relented and announced that this 121-year-old base will remain in active military status. In fact, it got an appropriation for new military construction.

How did this happen? Over the years the base had been reduced from 7,898 acres to a mere 119. The Army figured it would save $792,000 a year if it closed the old base, though closing it would cost $2.56 million. Now a Senator who over the years had become the champion of this base (in his district) challenged these figures. He called for a General Accounting Office audit in 1979, claiming that the Army had underestimated the costs of closing the base. The GAO came back with an estimate of $580,000 in annual savings if the base were closed, with a closing expense of $2.65 million—only $90,000 more than the Army had estimated.

From his seat on the Defense Appropriations Subcommit-

tee, this Senator wrote a section in the fiscal 1981 appropriations bill denying the Army the money to close the base. Instead, the Army was instructed to come up with an
"alternative uses study" for the fort. At this point, the Defense
Department gave up. There was no further proposal for closing the base. And in the fiscal 1984 budget, the Senator got
$910,000 to construct a new entryway processing station, giv-
ing the obsolete base still another lease on life.

Tornado in a Teapot

Since 1979, officials at the National Oceanic and Atmospheric Administration have been trying to close some of
the lowest-priority weather stations—part-time facilities
with no radar or other equipment, facilities not needed for
the national forecasting system. These weather stations provide no information or service that is not readily available
from one of the fifty-two regional offices. Many of the redundant facilities are rural offices that do no more than adapt
forecasts from the regional office for local use and provide
community liaison.

Congress rejected closing these offices in 1979 and 1980. In
1982, the agency tried again. It proposed a plan to close 38 of
the 234 local weather stations, all with five or fewer employees, at a saving of $1.8 million. The closings would affect
85 of the 5,000 jobs in the National Weather Service—that is,
only 1.5 percent of them. Congress agreed to close 18.

Now one of those local weather stations—staffed by only a
single employee—was located in a town of less than 3,000,
whose Representative in Congress is a member of the Appropriations Committee.

Even though Congress had approved 18 closings, this
member of Congress was determined to prevent it. This member opened fire on March 3, 1982, as Commerce Secretary
Malcolm Baldrige appeared before a House Appropriations

Subcommittee. The Representative described the weather stations as "marked for dehumanization" and told the Secretary that they should be cutting the "real fat" out of the budget rather than doing away with those eighteen stations. This member claimed that the "only protection the community has from tornadoes is the eyes and judgement of the human beings" assigned to the weather station there.

But Mr. Baldrige explained that the weather station provided no service not already available from the regional center, and that even if the regional center missed a gathering storm, there was no way to forecast it locally.

Next, the Representative suggested that the agency's budget of $14.4 million for automating local weather service be spent instead to keep the eighteen part-time stations open. When Secretary Baldrige disagreed, the Representative called for separate hearings on each closing. The Secretary explained that such hearings would drag out the process probably to the year 2000.

The Representative had had enough: "This is a red-hot issue. The authorizing committees in the House and the Senate are working on it. There is going to be a subcommittee meeting this afternoon. I am not only going to appear before this subcommittee, I am going to appear before the full Appropriations committee. I am going to appear before the authorizing committee. I am going to present my case when the supplemental budget comes up . . . when any reconciliation or resolution comes up. I am going to fight for it all the way, because I think you are making a ghastly mistake."

Later that year, Congress reversed its decision to close the eighteen local weather stations. Instead it voted $1.8 million to keep all thirty-eight local stations open. In 1983, when the agency returned to Congress, this time with a proposal to close sixty-three weather service offices for savings of $3.8 million, Congress rejected the entire package out of hand. No closings were proposed for 1984, and the local weather stations are still operating at unnecessary cost to the taxpayers.

Every Sunday, Wednesday, and Friday at 9:05 P.M., The Cardinal glides out of Washington, D.C.'s, Union Station heading for Chicago. It arrives twenty-one hours later, after traveling 904 miles through the hills of Western Maryland, the mountains of West Virginia, and the rolling farmland of Ohio and Indiana. The fare is $76 one way in coach, or $157 for a sleeper. The fare covers only 60 percent of the train's operating costs, in part because The Cardinal's ridership is low—it averaged only 142 riders per trip in 1982. The deficit of $2.2 million in that year was covered from taxpayer funds. Things were worse in 1980 and 1981, when revenues covered less than half the costs, and subsidies totalled $13.4 million for the two years, that is, three times the loss of the previous year.

In late 1981, Amtrak officials decided to sideline The Cardinal, along with a number of money-losing long-distance passenger trains. The International between Seattle and British Columbia was taken out of service, as were The North Star between Duluth and Chicago and The Inter-American between Houston, San Antonio, and Laredo, to name a few.

Yet one Senator decided that his constituents deserved to have the services of The Cardinal, even though apparently few of them used it. When the 1982 Transportation Appropriations bill came before the Senate, he moved to get The Cardinal back on track by adding language in the bill that said "notwithstanding any other provision of law," Amtrak "shall provide through rail passenger service between Washington, D.C., and Chicago via Cincinnati."

A Senate colleague tried to strike the sentences, noting that the train didn't meet the minimum ridership that Congress had required to continue a train and its subsidy. "If we keep this in the appropriations bill, we are saying that there is one train that is preferred," he said, "even though it does not meet any criteria that we set in statute." He pointed out that "there is no other train in this nation that is designated by law to run." But his logic failed, and The Cardinal still shuttles between Washington and Chicago.

Congress even tells some federal agencies who they can hire and fire. The Administrator of the Veterans Administration, under a 1981 law, must now submit a detailed plan for any reorganization that will affect as few as three employees. Plus, the Administrator must submit the plan to Congress on the same day the President submits the next fiscal year's budget. Since that happens in February, it gives Congress until the next October 1, when the new fiscal year starts, to review the VA reorganization plan.

In the 1982 Supplemental Appropriations Act for the Department of Energy, Congress got right down to numbers. In the bill, it allocated to the Assistant Secretary for Conservation and Renewables exactly 353 employees. The bill went even further, telling the Secretary where most of them would go. It said 154 of the employees would work in conservation research and development, while 180 would work in state and local conservation activities.

Time and time again we see the same sort of thing, often with absurd results. When the Executive Branch tries to save money by eliminating things that have a relatively low national priority, inevitably this will affect some region or locality somewhere. The area's Senators and Representatives mobilize and mostly they win. The plan is scrapped, not because the cut doesn't make sense, but because our political process allows local interests to take precedence over national ones, resulting in waste, inefficiency, and higher costs to the taxpayer.

Here are a few more brief examples of Congressional interference.

1. A Representative inserts language into an appropriations bill to exempt his state from paying back misspent Federal funds.

groups. Each of the 535 Congressmen finds it much safer politically to push for his region's special interests rather than
national benefits that may not be immediately apparent, especially not to voters back home.

A public opinion poll conducted nationwide during the
summer of 1983 found, for instance, that 31 percent of those
sampled disapproved of the way Congress was handling its
job, while only 10 percent disapproved of the way their own
Congressional representatives were handling themselves in
office. Those 21 percentage points of difference may reflect as
well the same sort of ambivalence many Americans feel when
they attempt to assess the impact of spending decisions made
in Washington. If a Senator agrees that yes, Fort Obsolete
should be shut down, with 200 home folks losing their jobs in
order to help cut the national budget deficit, his courage is
not likely to be rewarded at the ballot box. The national issue—the budget deficit—doesn't have as strong and vocal a
constituency in the home region as does the military base.
Fort Obsolete excites immediate outcries, because you're
talking about these local people's livelihoods, even if it's only
a few people. (However, if we let the deficit go along as it is,
we'll be talking about many more jobs, when the national
economic consequences come home to roost not far off in the
future.)

If we're not watchful and critical, statesmanship devolves
into grubby politicking. The public interest is sacrificed to
private interests. It's a matter of the incentives offered by the
political system, for the kind of statesmanship that entails
courageously blending the multitudes of private interests to
the public good.

Here's how the system works. The President each February
submits to Congress his budget, which is his estimate of how
much money it will take to run the Federal government, including new spending for the fiscal year beginning that October. Then the Congressional Appropriations Subcommittees

divide up the budget. For instance, the Appropriations Sub-committee on Transportation takes charge of the budget for the Department of Transportation. Over the next eight months, the Secretary of Transportation and the administrators of the different agencies in the Department will testify before the Subcommittee. There, they will be asked to explain and justify why they want more money (though recently many have been asked to tell why they want less).

In such a setting, each Congressman has the opportunity to influence national spending in ways that benefit his own district, ignoring the national interest. He is encouraged to do this by colleagues and agency chiefs all too willing to accept this "minor" change or that one so the whole spending bill gets passed.

The Urban Mass Transportation Administration may or may not want to spend funds for a certain subway system in a particular city. Or the Federal Aviation Administration may want money to expand an airport in one community or close an airport tower in another. Well, Congress can require the Mass Transportation Administration to build a subway wherever Congress wants it, or require it to keep a control tower open. It does so by voting money to operate a facility, whether the agency wants it operated or not. It can insert language in spending bills that keeps a facility open. In the process, each member of Congress balances potential conflicts between the public interest and the special interests of his constituencies.

A tool of this political trading is the legislative rider. This is language written into a bill that has no direct bearing on the main thrust of the legislation, and so merely rides along with it. The rules of both House and Senate supposedly bar legislative riders, but these rules are often ignored—to the serious disadvantage of the American taxpayer. Congress uses the rider not merely to impose spending directions and requirements on the Executive Branch, but also to direct management operations or even override management decisions.

In May 1983, for example, the Department of Agriculture's Farmers Home Administration announced plans to move its office from one city to another in the same state. The agency's appropriations bill, which came out in June of that year, didn't specifically bar the move but, in reports accompanying the bill, the House and Senate Agricultural Appropriations Subcommittees said it should not be done.

The Farmers Home Administration retorted that the report language was not binding, and it would proceed with the move. Congressional reaction was swift. A supplemental appropriations bill for fiscal 1983, to allow extra money for a number of programs, was being considered in July. A clause was added that said none of the funds appropriated by that or any other Act could be used to relocate the FmHA office in question.

Now if the President disagreed with that rider, he could not show his disapproval without vetoing the rest of the appropriations bill. He has only the right to accept an entire bill or veto it entirely. If he had vetoed that Supplemental Appropriations Bill, the veto would have cut needed funds from the Food Stamp Program, the Health and Human Services Department, the Food and Drug Administration, the Department of Justice, and a host of others. So no matter how strong his disapproval of the rider, the President had no real option but to approve the entire bill, including the rider, and this is what he did. It's Congressional blackmail.

When a Bill Was a Bill

The signers of the Constitution didn't really mean to so hamstring the President. When they gave the President the power to veto a legislative bill from Congress, they thought of the term "bill" in much narrower terms than it has come to signify. In the early stages of our government, a bill was concerned only with a single, specific subject, which had to be clearly labeled in the bill's title.

But over the years, Congress has vastly enlarged the number and scope of unrelated subjects that together comprise a bill. Nowadays, a single appropriations bill may cover several unrelated departments, agencies, and programs. Obviously, the President is thus deprived of the chance to veto proposed legislation on a single subject.

One way to repair this failure of our political culture would be to give the President an "item" veto, so he could sign major legislation without also approving all sorts of dubious or unwise riders hooked onto the bill like barnacles on a ship's hull. If Congress is adamant, it could always override the veto. The item veto works well in the forty-three American states where Governors have it. Congress naturally fears that giving the President an item veto would impinge on its powers, and it has repeatedly refused to even give him the less restrictive "line item" veto—one that allows selective vetoes of "line items" in money appropriations bills only.

In the 1960s, it was accepted to leave well enough alone. Then we tolerated whatever inefficiencies resulted from legislative riders and similar actions simply because the budget deficits averaged a "manageable" $6 billion a year. Now, with deficits approaching $200 billion annually, we need to cure this flaw in our political process, to better enable the government to come to grips with its overspending. Indeed, we calculate cost savings of about $7.8 billion over three years—plus an extra $1.1 billion in revenue generation—if cost-reduction programs such as military base closings now blocked by Congress were carried out.

Our recommendation of a Presidential item veto in no way impinges on Congress's constitutional rights and obligations. Rather it would add a constructive element that could lead to a significant reduction in management ineffectiveness.

The dimensions of the challenge were clearly drawn in remarks made by a leading Congressman to the House of Representatives just before Congress adjourned in 1983. He said, "We have confessed to an already doubting nation that we are ruled by political fear rather than economic courage."

Chapter 4

A Private Sector Survey

The Buck (=29¢) Stops Here

When Ronald Reagan moved into the Oval Office in 1981, he was faced with a national debt of $794 billion and a $57.9 billion budget deficit that would, over the next two years, increase by almost 90 percent annually—that is, almost doubling in size each year. Early on, the President hired some new Inspectors General to seek out waste. Their efforts simply highlighted how massive the problem of waste in government was. Meanwhile, fraud such as tax cheating and unpaid debts to the government had escalated beyond the government's ability to keep pace. Besides the Inspectors General, President Reagan also set up the President's Council on Integrity and Efficiency, the Cabinet Council on Management and Administration, and Reform 88, which aimed to cut down costs; eliminate waste, fraud, and abuse; and improve the overall management practices, procedures, methods, and systems of government. While these Presidential initiatives have substantially improved many aspects of Federal operations, it was clear that more needed to be done. The question became how best to attack the massive waste and inefficiency which seemed to pervade virtually all governmental activities. The answer came from a success story some fifteen years earlier.

48

California, Inc.

In 1967, as Ronald Reagan began his term of office in the Governor's Mansion at Sacramento, California was running a state deficit of $500,000 a day.

No private company could long tolerate a $500,000 per day excess of expenses over revenues. A corporation cannot operate with a continuing and growing deficit. If you don't operate efficiently, continually watching costs while giving customers the best possible products and services, you lose money, investors sell your stock, and ultimately you go out of business.

Governor Reagan decided to call on successful California businessmen—corporate executives and management experts—to look through the state government and find out where tax money could be saved by applying the common-sense techniques of good business management.

Governor Reagan's California cost-cutting commission enlisted some 250 businessmen volunteers and let them analyze the government's files. Their analysis took 117 days. They uncovered some 2,200 possible savings ideas. The Governor was later able to enact almost 75 percent of the businessmen's efficiency recommendations, saving California taxpayers hundreds of millions of dollars. The plan had been a success. The commission's work materially helped Ronald Reagan bring California from a $180-million yearly deficit to a budget surplus.

If It Worked Once, Could It Work Again?

So President Reagan went back to his earlier success in California. He called in his closest advisors and suggested they all try it again, this time on a national scale. The more politically oriented of his advisors were dubious. Real budget-cutting proposals are political dynamite. For every expenditure, whether sheer waste or absolutely essential, there's a recipient, and he or she tends to react strongly when benefits are reduced or taken away.

Despite the skepticism of some of his advisors, the President went forward with his plans. Certainly there were precedents, going as far back as the Taft Commission on Economy and Efficiency in 1910, and up to the 1977 Carter Reorganization Project. But the Federal government was overdue for a more in-depth analysis. Immediately, the criticism began: Government, it was pointed out, performs roles that have no counterpart in private enterprise. You can't compare government to a private business. Can you imagine a private corporation running a criminal court? Justice can't be administered on a profit-making basis. Then too, there are times when the public decides that a government ought to subsidize some services—medical care and education, for example—at a loss.

The President's idea was not to change any of that. It was simply to have expert businessmen take a close-up look at those important functions that are comparable in both the public and private sectors. A government agency hires and (rarely) fires people; keeps (or pretends to keep) accounting books; uses (or rather misuses) computers; manages (or rather mismanages) bank accounts; borrows and lends money (lends money it doesn't have to people who can't afford to borrow; not surprisingly, the government doesn't get back much of the money it lends); buys and sells materials (when the government sells something it usually winds up costing the taxpayers money); produces reports; and does dozens of the same things a private corporation does.

The government has already become, in effect, the world's largest conglomerate, consuming a steadily increasing share of the nation's output.

The Federal government is the world's largest: power producer, insurer, lender, borrower, hospital system operator, landowner, tenant, holder of grazing land, timber seller, grain owner, warehouse operator, ship owner, and truck fleet operator. The Federal government employs 2.8 million civilians and 2.1 million servicemen. It spent nearly $796 billion in fiscal 1983, a quarter of all the nation's output, as measured by the Gross National Product. The Federal government owns a third of the U.S. land mass and occupies 2.6 billion square feet of office space—equivalent to all the office space in America's ten largest cities, multiplied by four. The Federal government owns and operates 436,000 nonmilitary vehicles. It has over 17,000 computers, 332 accounting systems, and over 100 payroll systems.

However, while many of the functions performed by business and government are comparable, there is an important difference. Business has to perform those functions efficiently and profitably if it is to survive. That is the discipline of the marketplace and competition ensures that an individual company simply cannot afford to maintain a bloated payroll or mismanage its cash or pay more than it has to for the goods and services it purchases. In addition, the private sector company cannot afford to maintain obsolete computers or adopt an accounting system that cannot keep score (that is really what an accounting system is—a scoreboard to tell you whether you are ahead or behind, winning or losing). The government, meanwhile, does not have to make a profit. It does not even have to keep score since it cannot lose. It can print or borrow money to offset its losses (deficits) and it has no competitors. If it has no competitors and it can print or borrow as much money as it needs, what incentive does the government have to efficiently and effectively perform its functions? *None.*

American taxpayers, however, allow their government to escape the discipline of the marketplace. We have given government a free hand to mismanage our affairs. We have done this by voting for Congressmen and Senators who have no conception of the terrible consequences that deficit spending will bring. Or if they do understand, they don't care; they just want to stay in office. This is a democratic country; if things are not as we wish, we have no one to blame but ourselves. What most of us don't consider is that, once government has spent our money, taxpayers ultimately have to pay up, whether it's now (through tax revenues) or later (through the interest on government borrowing—forget ever paying back the principal; just meeting the interest payments on this huge and growing debt virtually guarantees that we'll be spending more and more of our time working for the Federal government).

Why Me?

How was I chosen to head the survey looking into this giant enterprise? As I have said many times, I don't know.

The President and his advisors reviewed the names of likely candidates to head a new cost study commission. The President called and asked whether I would consent to take the job. I said yes right away. I agreed without a second thought because naturally I consider it a personal honor and a duty to serve the President and our country. Most people would. And for years I've watched and criticized increased Federal spending, and this was an opportunity to substitute action for words.

I did have some qualms. I just wasn't sure how much could realistically be accomplished by this sort of project. Would this be another commission report to be filed away and gather dust? How could I in good conscience ask some of the highest-ranking and busiest executives in America to put so much time and effort into a deficit-cutting study when everybody "knew" the budget couldn't be cut? There was another consideration: President Reagan said on the phone that he wanted this to be entirely a volunteer effort, as it had been in California. The government would not contribute a cent. He asked that civic-minded corporations donate money and materials and—most important—their best managerial talent. That was asking a lot, I thought. How many millions would have to be raised? What would the contributors have to show for their donations? Would the commission do any good?

President Reagan invited me to the White House for the signing of the executive order setting up the commission. It was to be officially known as the President's Private Sector Survey on Cost Control. After the formal ceremony, when the reporters and photographers had left, the President explained in detail what he wanted our mission to be. We were to recruit the best management people in the private sector and set them to the task of doing on-site studies of all the major departments and agencies that make up the executive branch.

We began at once. The first big task was to recruit 160 of the best and brightest of American corporate talent, the chief executives of the nation's leading corporations, for our Executive Committee. One main criterion for selecting the members was their expertise in sound management of large enterprises, as evidenced by their own performance in business. The other main criterion was their willingness to be actively involved. One columnist noted at the time that "Grace certainly will not allow his commission to become a sort of friendly club for tired tycoons wanting to do a little good for their country in their spare time." Our committee members would confirm that his commentary turned out to be correct.

Due to the personnel and conflict-of-interest clearances that everybody had to undergo, and other administrative paperwork, the commission did not get under way until June of 1982. By then, a staff of more than 2,000 corporate volunteers had been assembled.

The War on Waste

We signed up business leaders like Frank Cary, Chairman of the Executive Committee of IBM; Amory Houghton, Chairman, Corning Glass Works; Roger Milliken, President of Milliken Company; Willard C. Butcher, Chairman of The Chase Manhattan Bank; Professor Lawrence Fouraker of the Harvard Business School; Joseph Alibrandi, President of Whittaker Corporation; Robert Beck, Chairman of Prudential Insurance Company; Clifton Garvin, Chief Executive Officer of Exxon; Robert Galvin, Chairman of Motorola; Lewis Preston, Chairman of Morgan Guaranty Trust Co.; and Donald Keough, President of Coca-Cola. That's just a small sample. The list reads like an honor roll of American leadership, and I am most proud to have served with such outstanding people.

What are their politics? I don't know, or care. No thought was given to politics in putting together the Commission. I literally didn't know where 90 percent of the Executive Committee members stood politically. I only know that they were with us all the way in this effort. As I have mentioned, I've been a lifelong registered Democrat myself. The desire to cut Federal spending and eliminate the deficit cuts across all political lines.

We set up a fifty-plus person Management Office in Washington to oversee survey operations. The Chief Operating Officer was J. P. Bolduc, formerly vice president and a partner with Booz, Allen and Hamilton, the management consulting firm, and now a senior vice president at Grace. Our Deputy Director was Janet Colson, who was Special Assistant to the President and served as liaison between the White House and the Survey. A dozen senior management consultants and executives temporarily, and at considerable cost, set aside their professional practices to join the Management Office and work on the Survey.

They served as "desk officers," directing the day-to-day work of more than 2,000 corporate volunteers who manned the front lines—accountants, line officers, management and financial experts on loan from large corporations. We grouped them into thirty-six task forces. Some twenty-two task forces focused on single departments or agencies, and fourteen of them focused on major functions cutting across all departments and agencies, on topics such as personnel management and procurement.

Here's how each task force worked, using the Treasury Task Force as an example: First, project managers and core staff people were thoroughly briefed on the workings of the government in general and the Treasury Department in particular. This stage included initial interviews with top Treasury officials and the preparation of a bibliography of reports and materials to study. Department spending and income trends over the past twenty years were arrayed and examined.

We were amazed to learn that the Federal government keeps no historical record of its spending by line item—things such as utility costs, phone bills, travel—and, as mentioned earlier, we had to compile this data ourselves, with an equivalent of ten man-years of work. This kind of historical spending data is essential to identifying possible excesses in any cost-cutting analysis, so it is no wonder that past attempts at cutting costs have been less than successful. Hundreds of General Accounting Office, Office of Management and Budget, and Inspectors General reports were reviewed and analyzed.

Next, the Treasury Task Force did extensive interviews with senior Treasury officials and studied all relevant materials to identify which specific issues to analyze in depth. Once these were determined, task force staffing was arranged, schedules were worked out and work plans submitted. Thus prepared, the task force members surveyed the areas to which they had been assigned. They looked for targets where cost-cutting measures would be most effective in providing important long-term savings.

We tried to avoid the trap of recommending only near-term solutions to problems. The entire appropriations process suffers from a short-term perspective that ensures that politically palatable compromises, often with costly, unnecessary long-term results, will be adopted. For example, "stretching out" weapons-buying programs can save money in the short term, but it adds to the long-term total costs. I emphasize our belief that the near-term budget-reducing potential of a recommendation is simply inadequate as a basis for measuring its merit. No one would do that with his or her own money.

Finally, the task force spent weeks verifying its facts and analyses, preparing a plan for putting its recommendations into effect, and writing up its recommendations. After all the task force recommendations were in and the reports written, around Christmas of 1983, we condensed them into a two-volume Final Report to the President.

Our labors, which extended over almost two years, produced some 47 in-depth reports, which, including the Final Report, totaled more than 21,000 pages, with an additional 1.5 million pages of supporting documentation. Three-year savings of $424.4 billion in spending cuts and revenue enhancements were recommended, ranging in size from about $500,000 to $58.9 billion. All this work was done at a donated cost of $76 million in manpower, equipment, and materials. The only thing the government paid for was Ms. Colson's salary. The rest came from the private sector.

From day one, we were concerned with avoiding even the appearance of a conflict of interest. All members of the Executive Committee were cleared by the White House Office of Legal Counsel. Then, those members of the Executive Committee who were assigned to serve as task force co-chairs were also cleared for conflicts of interest by the departments and agencies they would be investigating, which is the primary reason why it took so long to get started. Everybody else who worked for the commission was subject to our strict internal rules against conflict of interest.

None of those checks and balances stopped some Congressional critics from accusing us of conflict of interest anyway. Rep. Charles Dingle of Michigan, patron saint of the Environmental Protection Agency, claimed that our task force should be locked out of its offices. Rep. William Ford, also of Michigan, was even more vociferous. He was particularly put out by our uncovering excesses in the Civil Service system. Rep. Ford is chairman of the House Post Office and Civil Service Committee, and it is the responsibility of his committee to have corrected such excesses in the past; instead he has been one of the chief supporters of these excesses.

It is interesting to note that members of Congress generally insist that there is no connection between their votes on legislation and the campaign contributions they receive from special interest groups. I recently read a newspaper article, headed "Coincidence dept.: vote the right way and get the dough," which noted the remarkable coincidence in the timing of campaign contributions from the insurance industry and Representatives' votes on the bill to equalize insurance premiums and benefits for men and women. I'm willing to give Congress the benefit of the doubt—no conflict of interest here. Unfortunately, they're generally unwilling to extend the same courtesy to unpaid volunteers who simply wanted to help improve our government's disastrous financial condition, for which Congress must accept substantial responsibility.

Rigid rules sometimes prevented us from making the best use of the corporate leaders who volunteered for the Executive Committee. For instance, Frank Cary, Chairman of the Executive Committee of IBM, knows more about computers than just about anybody. But government officials said if he headed our data processing task force, there might be the *appearance* of a conflict of interest. Somehow IBM might get a special advantage. That seemed pretty remote but, in the end, Frank Cary had to be assigned to the task force on the Department of Housing and Urban Development. Must it be a criminal offense to know something about the subject you're dealing with in government?

The policy versus efficiency issue was also a major problem for our survey. Congress seems to look on almost any administrative change in the Federal government as a "policy matter." You have the Chairman of the Securities and Exchange Commission forced to reinstate employees he had earlier dismissed as unnecessary. Some Congressmen turned it into a political issue and demanded their reinstatement. So beyond conflict of interest, we were also attacked for allegedly delving into government policy. But policy was not our interest at all. That's for the various branches of government to determine. Policy is the expression of the people's will through the democratic process, at least insofar as the process works properly. We did not even pretend to say how the government should use its resources in defense, education, welfare, highways, and other matters of national interest. We assumed as a given that present policy would continue. Whether it will or not was not of concern to us as a commission.

We did look at how well policy was executed. But we were only concerned with efficiency. The decision of the government to give out food stamps, for example, was not our concern. Our purpose was to see how well the government was performing in getting those stamps out at the least cost.

It is admittedly difficult to draw the line between operations and policy. For example, our report on subsidized programs recommended that the government poverty figures be revised to include "in-kind" income such as food stamps and housing subsidies. That just makes good sense. If someone's

income is counted as, say, $4,800 a year, but that person gets
$200 worth of food stamps a month and a housing subsidy of
$250 a month, then it would make sense to consider that
person's income as being $10,200 a year, including $5,400 in
food stamps and housing subsidies. But if you do that, then
you might disqualify that person for some other kind of aid—
for instance, a subsidized loan or free dental care. Perhaps
that person should be disqualified from one or both programs, but whether he should be or not is a policy question.
The problem is the government doesn't know how much any
particular individual or business is receiving in subsidies. So
it can't determine what policy to choose, and our recommendations were to provide that information, not to determine policy.

These sorts of problems are not uncommon in government. Earlier study groups such as the Hoover Commission
back in the late 1940s and mid-1950s had these same diffi-
culties. Few things can be colored in black or white. There are
many shades of gray, and it would have been counterproductive to abandon our studies to appease the critics. The fact is
that the blurred lines occasionally provided those who
wanted to discredit our efforts with a wedge to criticize our
results.

What We Found: The Highlights

In the following pages, I want to briefly summarize
the broad categories of government inefficiency we found. But
these examples represent only the tip of the iceberg in regard
to what our Survey uncovered. In a word, the Federal government is run "horribly."

The Information Gap. Huge quantities of numbers are
generated every day by the government, but little of it is processed and organized into useful information. Lots of data,
little information. For example, the Air Force Logistics Com-

mand produces six million pounds of paper a year, which represents a stack thirty-three miles high, but provides little usable information. In many government agencies, they don't even know what information they need to manage themselves; data are incomplete, inconsistent, and often just wrong. You can't manage an organization without having the proper information and knowing what it means.

Automating for Efficiency. The government's numbers are generated on computers that are so old that in at least half the cases the manufacturers refuse to provide service for them. The Federal government uses more than 17,000 computers, more than half of which are obsolete. Most of them are incompatible since each agency buys its own computers without adequate coordination. Of the 250,000 government computer personnel, many are poorly qualified or anxious to leave their jobs, because the government pays uncompetitive salaries for their skills. Most of the talented data processing specialists who came to the government in the mid-1960s have left (see chapter 8).

Managing Money. The Federal government handles some $6.8 billion in transactions a day—that's equivalent to 215.6 years of seconds handled in dollars every day—but despite these enormous sums the government is years behind the private sector in developing modern budgeting and accounting systems. Nor is it familiar with the common business techniques of cash, loan, and debt management. Each department uses its own accounting systems (there are 332 incompatible accounting systems), making accurate government-wide analysis impossible. The government has issued, backed, or sponsored $848 billion in loans outstanding, but lacks adequate controls and thus is highly vulnerable to substantial losses due to error or outright fraud. Government budgeting is mainly concerned with getting next year's spending levels approved, while, in the private sector, results versus what was budgeted in previous years are also examined. Compared to private business, Federal budgeting is done in a vacuum, where past budgets are forever forgotten, and there is little accountability. The Federal government has an annual cash flow of $1.7 trillion; however, cash-management procedures are so poor that money sits idle in non-interest-bearing accounts, costing taxpayers billions of dollars each year.

Will the Real Budget Please Stand Up? The Federal budget greatly understates the true level of Federal activity. First, the government practice of "offsetting" (deducting from spending) amounts collected from loan repayments and the like distorts the picture of actual spending levels. Then, the "off-budget" Federal Financing Bank hides more government spending by offering the Federal agencies a "back door" to the Treasury. What this means is that $16.2 billion of Federal spending is just not counted in government statistics for fiscal 1984. Government loan guarantees and the credit of government-sponsored enterprises are not adequately disclosed in the budget. If you take all these hidden items into account, actual Federal commitments including loans for fiscal 1984 total $1.8 trillion, more than double the $854-billion amount shown in the budget.

The Impact of Not Buying Prudently. In fiscal 1982, a typical year, the Federal government bought $159 billion in goods and services. Sixty billion dollars of that went for military weapons, the remainder for various goods and services across government. Some $41 billion worth of inventories were stored in hundreds of locations around the country. But the 130,000 Federal procurement personnel—government shoppers—find it difficult to recognize a bargain when they see one. First, they are entangled in over 80,000 pages of procurement regulations, plus 20,000 pages of revisions each year. Besides that, they work with inaccurate information, and their buying is often poorly planned and uncoordinated. You've read stories of the government paying $91 for a 3-cent hardware store screw. What is even more worrisome is that the big items—aircraft, turbines, rockets—are not bought with any greater concern for how much is paid out. The opportunity for fraud and abuse is immense. It is shameful but true that some government contractors get rich by hugely overcharging the government.

Managing the Government's Facilities. At the end of fiscal 1980, the latest year anybody counted, the Federal government estimates that it owned real estate worth at least $104 billion. That's probably understated, since it includes 744 million acres valued at only $13.44 per acre—just add another $20 an acre and the government's land holdings go up in value by $14.9 billion. The government keeps no current inventory of its property or how much it is worth. The General Services Administration, in charge of leasing government office space, gets charged as much as $7 per square foot more than prevailing rates because of its complex leasing regulations. The government's fleet of 318,000 cars and trucks (excluding Postal Service vehicles), the largest in the world, is used 64 percent less than the 25,000 yearly mileage rate that private rental firms consider efficient. There is no centralized information on these vehicles. The sticker price on a Volkswagen is $14,800. Multiply 318,000 vehicles times $14,800 and you come up with $4.7 billion worth of vehicles. And this we mismanage!

The Cost of Not Watching the Store. The Federal government doesn't pay enough attention to the little things—housekeeping, travel, freight, mailing, printing, and so on; it doesn't even know how much many of these functions cost in total. They never tote this up and never look back. The result is excessive costs amounting to tens of billions of dollars a year. But there's no incentive to watch these activities. In fiscal 1982, the government spent $4.8 billion on employee travel. Because of the amount of travel, the government ought to have an in-house travel service, as most corporations do, to negotiate discounts and to efficiently book employee travel. But again, nobody in Washington cares about details. It isn't their money that they're wasting—it's yours.

Opportunities for Increasing Revenue. The Federal government offers more than fifteen hundred goods and services to the public—pamphlets, camp grounds, firewood, and soil analysis, for example. A lot of these items are just given away. Even with the things the government offers for sale, the price doesn't begin to cover costs. That's permissible if there's rational policy. But what sort of policy is served by giving away firewood (not necessarily to poor people), for instance? A total of $235 million of it was given away in 1982. The Defense Department charges $6,000 an hour for the use of its wind tunnels, but NASA charges $2,000 an hour for its wind tunnels. Naturally, private industry uses the NASA wind tunnels more. Government officials generally are confused about how much to charge and why.

Getting More Use Out of the Private Sector. Government is best at providing for the nation's defense and domestic security. But there are a great many things the government now does that could be handled by the private sector more effectively and at less cost. For instance, when the Veterans Administration fills all its nursing home beds, it contracts out for additional ones. In fiscal 1981, the average cost for patient care in a VA nursing home was $109 per day. In a private facility it was $45, or less than half as much. The government set up military commissaries in the last century to provide food for soldiers in isolated outposts. Now there are 238 of them in the U.S., including six in a wild frontier outpost like Washington, D.C. These government grocery stores, which cost $758 million to operate in 1983, no longer serve any justifiable purpose for servicemen.

From the many problems and deficiencies we uncovered,

there are a few general problems that can be identified, which apply to just about every office of the Federal government:

1. There's no centralized management for financial and accounting operations. Though the Federal government accounts for nearly a fourth of all economic activity in the United States, no central office exists for developing and coordinating financial management practices. This is the basic cause of the government's problems with cash management, debt collection, inventory management, and financial reporting.

2. The lack of government-wide management information makes it difficult, almost impossible in fact, for Federal agencies to correct these inefficiencies. Since they don't have key indicators of their performance to judge themselves by, the Federal agencies tend to "control" their operations by standardizing every little procedure, and by churning out endless regulations.

3. The Federal government operates a revolving door for key management, so the agencies have little continuity in management. The average stay for political appointees in the agencies is only eighteen months. People leave before they have really learned their jobs. In the General Services Administration, for example, in the past ten years there have been nine administrators, ten deputy administrators, and fourteen different commissioners for procurement activities.

4. There are virtually no incentives for Federal personnel to seek the least costly, most efficient method of carrying out their functions. Without adequate incentives, the Federal employee cannot be expected to rise above mediocrity.

While the Survey enabled us to identify and suggest corrective action for specific problems, it was apparent to me, almost from the first, that the government was being poorly managed largely because of a lack of information.

Who's on First?

During my first few days as chairman of the President's Private Sector Survey on Cost Control, I had the opportunity to meet with President Reagan in Los Angeles. When our meeting concluded, the President said, "You know when I was governor of California there were more Federal employees out here than state employees. Would you please find out how many there are, where they work, and what they are all doing."

Back in Washington the next morning bright and early at 8:00 A.M. in the office that I had been given in the Executive Office Building, I tried to get the answer for the President. I checked with the Office of Management and Budget, one floor above, and OMB didn't have the answer. I checked all over Washington. No one had the answer. There is just no central source for that kind of information, which would be immediately available to any private-sector executive. The Federal government doesn't know how many offices it has or where they're located. We ended up checking through the yellow pages, thousands of them, looking for Federal government office listings, not only in California but all over the country. We wanted to know just how many offices the government maintained across the U.S. We never did find out but eventually we did learn that the government occupies four times all the office space in the ten largest U.S. cities.

At the start of our commission's work, we were appalled at the Federal government's lack of basic information on its own activities. Some records aren't kept for more than a year, and others are not kept at all. Some figures are available for certain years but not others.

Most government officials don't even know what the government is spending, because the government reports only "net outlays"—actual spending minus receipts.

Obligations, the most meaningful measure of government

65

spending, are $1.2 trillion in 1984, or 40 percent higher than estimated outlays of $854 billion. If our survey had addressed only outlays and looked at items with only near-term potential for deficit reductions, we would have short-changed the President, who had commissioned us to work like "tireless bloodhounds." Thus we spent the equivalent of more than ten man-years, reviewing fifteen thousand pages of Federal budget appendices, to put together what every private-sector executive has at his fingertips—a historical trend of line-item spending.

Further, not all of the deficit and debt of the Federal government is shown in the official figures. The $195.4 billion deficit reported in 1983 was just the "on-budget" deficit. It's a part of the game that's played with the Federal accounting systems—if you don't want an expenditure to show up, you move it into the "off-budget" account.

So, add $12.4 billion in off-budget outlays to the reported $195 billion deficit in 1983. Also, since the government doesn't bother to set up adequate reserves for the nearly $3 trillion in past service liabilities of future Civil Service and military pensions and Social Security, add the necessary annual charge of $186.1 billion required to amortize these liabilities over 40 years. With all the pieces added up, the true, actual deficit for 1983 was $393.9 billion, more than twice the reported $195.4 billion.

When we started our work, we tried to find out how many social programs there are. "Oh, about one hundred and twenty-five," we were told. Then we found the book *Fat City*, which describes hundreds of Federal programs that give money away for nonessential purposes—at the expense of taxpayers. We went back to the drawing board and spent six months looking into the question of how many government social programs there are. We found that there are 963 social programs. Somebody in Washington should have known the correct answer—125 was only 13 percent of the true total. That's what we found over and over again in Washington— somebody should know, but nobody does.

Chapter 5

The Privileged Elite

Working for Uncle

Look at the Federal government as an employer who has to compete with other employers, both public and private, to attract and retain workers. Private-sector companies are limited in the salaries and benefits they can afford to pay—they have to earn a profit. They want the best employees they can get, but they also need to control their costs.

They need to establish a balance, paying the salaries and benefits necessary to attract and retain qualified personnel while fulfilling their responsibility to earn profits and protect their shareholders' investment.

Where does the government fit into this spectrum? The government pays its employees at salary levels that are generally comparable to those in the private sector. However, the government provides fringe benefits that are 76 percent higher than in the private sector. The added cost is about $20 billion annually, while the government is "losing" hundreds of billions of dollars a year. Any private-sector company in this situation would face an angry shareholders' revolt. How does the U.S. Government get away with it? Why aren't Federal "shareholders" in revolt? In general, it is because they just don't know how generous they are in providing fringe benefits to Federal employees.

For example, Federal workers take 1.6 times the number of sick days and 1.4 times the number of vacation days that private-sector workers do. They retire earlier and get civilian and military pensions three and six times as great, respectively, as the best available in the private sector. In addition, they are just about immune to being fired.

When there is a reduction-in-force (in the private sector, that means workers being laid off or fired), Federal employees get to bump those with less seniority and, even though they may now hold positions with less responsibility and which are usually paid lower wages, they continue to receive their previous salaries, with full salary increases, for two years. Any privately owned operation that "bumped" people down while allowing them to retain their previous salaries and granting raises would have been nothing but a memory years ago.

These fringe benefits add up to a great deal. So the government doesn't lack for qualified candidates for its available positions. Of course, once you're hired, you have to put up with a system that encourages conformity and that discourages innovation. But you can retire at age 55 with a full pension, get four weeks' vacation after three years on the job, be entitled to thirteen days of sick leave annually, and, as a professional, expect to be promoted almost twice as quickly as your private-sector counterparts. All this while you were earning a salary approximately equivalent to that of private-sector workers.

Why have Federal benefits become so much more generous than those in the private sector? In the 1920s, it was felt that neither Civil Service nor military pay was competitive with salaries in private business. Rather than bite the bullet and raise pay, Congress decided to push costs far into the future (where current taxpayers and voters wouldn't notice them) by setting up an exceedingly generous pension system.

Then in 1962, Congress raised Federal pay, requiring that it be the same as that in private industry. But while Federal pay generally rose to equal and sometimes even exceed civilian pay, Federal pensions and benefits became progressively better than those in the private sector.

In 1982, average Civil Service pensions were over $17,600 a year for Federal Civil Service workers retiring after the normal thirty years of service. Including Social Security benefits, the average private-sector pension was $9,200—the average Civil Service pension 1.9 times as great.

To begin with, Federal pensions are larger than those paid by private-sector employers. But that's only for openers. In addition, the civil servant receives his benefits over a longer period of time since they can retire at an earlier age. They also receive full inflation protection while private-sector pensions are indexed at about 70 percent of inflation (that is, if you include Social Security—33 percent if you don't), and it becomes clear that Federal pensions are both generous and expensive ("generous" is really a bad term since that implies that we know what we're doing and actually very few taxpayers, that is, Federal employers, have any idea of the benefits they're providing their employees, that is, Civil Service workers).

Who pays for these pensions? Mostly, you do. While private-sector employees pay for about a third of their retirement benefits (primarily through Social Security payroll deductions), Civil Service workers pay for only 19 percent of theirs, and military personnel pay for only 13 percent (military personnel are covered by and pay for Social Security). Taxpayers are paying for over 80 percent of Federal pensions.

Congress has fully indexed these Federal pensions, so that when prices go up, so do Federal pensions. Between 1973 and 1979, inflation increased 60 percent, but Federal pensions rose by 84 percent. This happened because, between 1969 and 1976, the Federal cost-of-living adjustment rose not only by the rate of inflation, but by an extra percentage point. Not surprisingly, Civil Service pension costs grew from $2.8 billion in 1970 to $19.5 billion in 1982. If present trends continue, Civil Service pension costs alone, boosted by those cost-of-living adjustments (COLAs) will reach $261 billion by 1998.

These cost-of-living increases have outstripped Civil Service salary increases. For example, between 1968 and 1982 COLAs averaged 8.1 percent per year or 31 percent more than the 6.2 percent annual average increase in Civil Service white-collar salaries. A Civil Service worker who retired at the end of 1968, after 30 years of service, making $18,700 in his last year on the job, would be entitled to a 1968 pension of $10,000. By 1982, his pension would have risen to $29,800 a year, which is more than one and a half times his 1968 salary.

Under the same assumptions of age and service and adjusting the salary to reflect Federal pay increases, a 1982 retiree would receive a pension of $23,100. That's $6,700 a year or 22 percent less than the 1982 pension pay of the employee who retired from the Civil Service in 1968. Even though the 1968 retiree retired fourteen years earlier than the 1982 retiree, his pension is greater in 1982. Not only does this encourage early retirement, allowing Civil Service employees to get jobs in the private sector and pensions from the government at the same time, but it is very expensive and destroys morale. Imagine the feeling of an employee who remains on the job knowing that he will get less in salary increases than the cost-of-living adjustments granted to retirees.

The same disparity occurs in the military. Many military officers who retired in 1972 get higher retirement benefits, due to the cost-of-living adjustments, than officers of the same rank who retired in 1982. Some of those 1972 retirees are getting more money in retirement pay than equally ranked officers get in salary while on active duty. No private-sector employer can afford to match the generosity of Federal pension plans. Only 8 percent of the top private-sector corporations offer formal cost-of-living adjustments, and on average those adjustments equal only a third of the inflation rate.

71

The Federal pension plans are so expensive that, in order to match them, the private sector would have to come up with $450 billion a year, which is three times the total pretax profits of all nonfinancial U.S. corporations.

The Federal government runs some fifty different pension programs. In all, these fifty programs cover some 9.5 million Americans, over three million of whom are now getting benefits. About 98 percent of the costs of these pensions, roughly $34.4 billion in 1982, went to Civil Service and military employees.

However, the government can't afford the generosity of its pension plans and also chooses to ignore its actual costs. Beyond the $34 billion paid to civilian and military retirees in 1982, there were retirement benefits earned by current employees.

Current employees are earning retirement credits as they work. These costs should be accounted for by setting aside sufficient funds now to pay for their pension benefits in the future. In private business, with U.S. Government–approved pension plans, corporations are required by law to set aside funds sufficient to meet present and future pension obligations, and the Federal government monitors how these funds are invested. The Federal government, however, is exempt from such enforced prudence. The future pension obligations of the government for which no funds have been set aside add up to about $1.1 trillion. And this total has been increasing by about $100 billion a year. That's our legacy to future generations—a legacy I'm not anxious to explain to my children and grandchildren.

In 1982, the government would have had to put aside $41 billion each year for the next forty years to meet its existing future pension obligations. That's legally required of private-sector employers. Add that to the over $34 billion already spent, and the total Federal pension cost was $75 billion in

1982—about $1,000 per taxpayer each year, just to pay pension benefits to current and future Federal retirees.

Congressman Barber Conable warned that "we have constructed a Federal pensions system over the years which goes far beyond reasonable limits and threatens to overwhelm the American taxpayer."

If the problem is that serious, why hasn't something been done? The reasons are the same as those which answer why other inefficiencies exist in Federal operations. Federal employees and their unions are very powerful in Washington, and thus able to protect their interests. They know how to influence Congress and maintain their favorable pensions and benefits. In addition, nearly four hundred members of Congress are themselves receiving Federal pension benefits, and current members of Congress will receive benefits in the future. So, as you might expect, Congress does not act to reform the Federal pension system, since it is a beneficiary, and these lucrative benefits are much less visible than salary increases.

Another factor is the lack of adequate information. Over 50 percent of the $515-billion shortfall in reserves for the Civil Service Retirement System stems from the government's failure to accurately estimate the impact of salary increases and cost-of-living adjustments on pension benefits.

Also, defenders of the Federal pension systems seem to think that their purpose is somehow different from that of private-sector pension plans. They like to think of Federal pensions as salary continuation plans rather than retirement benefits. "Retirement" in the private sector, and as understood by most of us, means leaving the work force. This is usually not the case for Civil Service retirees, and certainly not the case for military retirees. They trade one job for another, going from one company (government) to another firm (the private sector). While private-sector pensions are meant to supplement loss of income, government pensions are more a continuation of wages since most Federal workers continue to be active in the work force. How can one use the term "pension" for someone receiving lifetime payments from the age of 40? Even at 55, we're talking about a relatively young and productive person voluntarily leaving Federal employment, but not necessarily the work force.

When you have special interests, pressure on Congress, lack of data, lack of public awareness, and vested Congressional interests, you have a race in which the public interest finishes dead last.

While outlays for military and civilian pensions have grown by more than 16 percent each year since 1970, membership has grown by only 5.4 percent. Expenses for Civil Service pensions alone increased 1,891 percent between 1960 and 1981, compared to the "mere" 568 percent increase in overall Federal spending during the period. It is fair to ask why pension costs are increasing so much more rapidly than the increase in membership in the systems. It doesn't make sense even when you include the increase in salaries over the past twelve years.

When you establish a pension system, you have to be very careful. A decision to grant a small increase in annual cost-of-living adjustments (COLAs) can mean billions of dollars in costs in future years if you have plans the size of the government's.

For example, a 1 percent increase in Civil Service COLAs means 11 percent in added costs (over $2 billion), while COLAs will add $28 billion to military pensions during 1983–1992.

Further, retirement at 55 costs an employer 1.7 times as much in lifetime benefits as retirement at 62. So you have to consider carefully at what age you allow employees to retire.

There just hasn't been enough attention paid to the price of continually pushing costs into the future. When you estab-

lish pension systems that allow a liberal benefit formula, retirement at a relatively early age, and provide full protection
against inflation, you should at least be prepared to pay the
price of the commitments you've made. Unlike most of us,
Congress never learned that there's no such thing as a free
lunch.

Retired at 37

The government's give-away-the-store-and-more pension plans entice Federal employees to retire early. In private
industry, the usual retirement age, if you want full pension
benefits, is 65, though some allow retirement at 62. In the
Civil Service, you can retire at 55. In the military, you can
retire as young as age 37—all you need is twenty years of
service. The cost-of-living adjustments in the government
pension plans give Federal workers every reason to take retirement as early as they can, simply because the pension
amounts rise faster than government salaries. If your salary
increases aren't large enough, try retirement—as did the 64
percent of all male Civil Service workers who retired before
age 62. That's 3.2 times the 20 percent of private-sector workers who retire before age 62.

A quarter of all military personnel retire from the service
in their thirties. The average enlisted man retires at age 41,
with twenty-one years of service. This is the age when private-
sector workers are just coming into their prime. But the
temptation to retire young is overwhelming. Here you are 37,
and you'll be getting a retirement check for the rest of your
life. You're still young enough to go into private industry now
and maybe double your retirement income. If you don't want
to work, the pension alone will probably support you.

Most retired Federal workers, both military and Civil Service, join the ranks of the "double-dippers." Having retired

from the government, they go to work in the private sector at least long enough to earn or increase their Social Security retirement benefits. If a Civil Service worker retires at age 55 and goes to work in private business for a few years, he'll get relatively higher Social Security benefits—meant for those workers who have earned low incomes throughout their careers.

Social Security benefits pay relatively more to low-income (or part-time and short-service employees) than to high-income employees, i.e., low income employees get high benefits relative to their low incomes. And since Social Security can not distinguish between long-service, low-pay positions and short-service, high-pay positions, Federal retirees get relatively high Social Security pensions. That is, they are treated as low-pay employees by Social Security, even though they are not.

The defenders of the military retirement system claim that early retirement is needed because military work is hazardous and the services need a youthful and vigorous force. This sounds reasonable, except that only 13 percent of those entering the military will stay long enough to benefit from these generous retirement provisions. Government estimates are that 92 percent of an enlisted man's career is spent in noncombat work (66 percent for officers). One study shows that a quarter of retiring military people were leaving clerical jobs. So even those soldiers who stay long enough to earn retirement benefits are mainly involved in routine functions, not in physically demanding work. Even for those involved in life-threatening situations, does it make sense to pay retirement benefits twenty years from now for risks taken today? It would be much better to compensate for risk by raising salaries—if that is necessary—than by paying benefits far in the future.

The youthful military retirement age also robs the armed

services of productivity. Military work has evolved from such laborious chores as cleaning and stripping M-1 rifles to positions requiring high-tech expertise with "smart" bombs, laser beams, and so forth. So it is a terrible waste to have personnel retire around age 40, just when they are getting good at what they've been trained—at great expense—to do.

Does it make sense to train a worker for twenty years, then tell him that he can have 50 percent of his salary, inflation adjusted, for the rest of his life?

Congressmen and the people who run the military retirement system insist that the youthful retirement ages are necessary to lure young, robust civilians to sign up. Yet numerous studies show that it is not the far-off prospect of retirement benefits that inspires a young man or woman to go into the military or any other field: It is the prospect of immediate cash and in-kind benefits that attracts and retains employees. Most people, particularly at 17 and 18, tend to think in the present, not twenty years in the future.

Unfortunately for the taxpayers, the cost of retirement at relatively youthful ages, both in the Civil Service and the military, is much higher than at normal retirement ages. Compared with the cost of retirement at age 65, the cost of an employee who retires at age 55 is twice as great. If he retires at age 40, it quadruples. Suppose a Federal employee is making $25,000 a year. If he is a Civil Service worker and retires at age 55 with 30 years of service, he will get $542,000 in lifetime retirement benefits. A private-sector employee would get $266,000 under similar conditions—the Civil Service retiree getting twice the private-sector average. If he is a military man who makes $25,000 a year and retires at age 39 after twenty years of service, he will get lifetime retirement benefits of $1,072,000, compared to $176,000 in the private sector. The military retiree's benefits are six times those offered by the best that business can afford. This is just one example of what the relative benefits are. At a salary level of $50,000 annually, Civil Service benefits are 2.7 times those of the private sector and military benefits, 6.7 times as great.

The young retirement ages for the Civil Service and especially for the military cannot be justified. If anything, youthful retirement is an especially wasteful loss of good people. We can save $8.2 billion over three years merely by raising the Federal retirement age to 62, the usual minimum in the private sector. And if we reduce the cost-of-living adjustments in Federal pension plans to what they are in the best corporate plans, we'll save another $10.2 billion over three years. That's $18.4 billion to be gained just by adjusting Federal retirement plans in these two areas.

The above comparisons highlight the major differences between Federal and private-sector pensions. These differences cost billions of taxpayer dollars annually, because the gap between the private-sector standards and the government policy is so vast.

But even little differences add up to billions in unnecessary and unwarranted costs. Take, for example, using accumulated sick leave to increase pension benefits. Unlike private-industry workers, Federal Civil Service workers can accumulate sick days without limit and then add the unused days onto their total service, which increases their retirement pay. Just by eliminating this practice, which is unmatched in the private sector, the taxpayers would save $300 million a year—an amount equal to the taxes paid by 135,000 median-income American families.

The Early Retirement Gambit

Separate from the matter of normal retirement ages set too low are the costs associated with Federal workers who retire before the normal retirement age. For instance, the normal retirement age in the private sector is 65 years, though in many companies you can retire with an unreduced pension at 62. If you retire before then, you lose 3 to 6 percent of your pension benefit for each year below 62 that you retire. This is called an actuarial reduction and, based on life-expectancy statistics, the early retiree will receive as much in lifetime benefits as the employee retiring at the normal retirement age. But if you retire below the 55-year-old minimum in the Civil Service, the reduction of your pension, based on an arbitrary formula, is only 2 percent. So those taxpayers not fortunate enough to be Federal employees are penalized 1.5 to 3.0 times as much as the civil servant when both take early retirement. How many other employers provide benefits to their employees that are substantially better than their own?

A Federal worker can take early retirement when his agency is undergoing a major reduction in force, a reorganization or transfer of function, or if a worker is let go (unless he was fired for misconduct). Eligibility requirements are twenty years of service at age 50 or twenty-five years of service at any age. Thus, in 1979, for example, the Energy Department reclassified more than half of its headquarters people. This qualified as a "reorganization" under government rules. So even though the "reclassification" affected only a handful of people, some 206 Energy Department employees took advantage of the loophole and retired early. They all had to be replaced, at considerable cost to the taxpayer.

In that same year, the Office of Personnel Management (OPM) reassigned some of its workers to new jobs. No one was let go. But since this reassignment officially qualified as a "reorganization," some 149 OPM employees decided to retire early at full benefits.

A year earlier, the Merit Systems Protection Board requested early retirement authority even before the board actually came into existence or anyone knew how it would be organized. Why the board asked for this early retirement authority is not clear. But once the Merit Systems Protection Board got it, seven officers of the board promptly took early retirement.

Nearly 10 percent of all Federal retirees have taken early retirement, because of the incentives built into Federal retirement programs. In 1982, voluntary early retirees were getting an average of $15,100 a year. Then don't forget the Social Security "double-dipping" that most of them will become eligible for. By the year 2000, some 100,000 additional Federal workers will have taken early retirement, adding further costs to the government in the form of higher pension outlays and from the loss of experienced workers.

Eliminating the Federal government's early retirement provisions can save us $3.7 billion over three years. More than $1.2 billion of the savings would come in the first year alone— equivalent to one year's Federal income taxes for 541,000 median-income American families. Removing early retirement rules would bring government pension benefits more into line with the best plans of private industry, and that is only fair.

Dishpan Hands Revisited

Recall the story of the "disabled" Federal worker with dishpan hands in chapter 1? Here's how it happens. As long as a Civil Service worker has five years of service, he or she can retire as disabled if unable to satisfactorily or efficiently perform one or more duties of the job, and is unable to be reassigned to a vacant post in the same agency at the same pay and grade. Thus, if a Federal worker can't do just one "essential function" of his or her job, the government counts the employee as "totally disabled."

In the private sector, to be eligible for disability retirement pay, usually an employee must be age 50 or older, worked with the company ten years or more, and be unable to do any job for which he or she is reasonably qualified. Even Social Security disability requires that the recipient be unable to do "any gainful employment."

Not unexpectedly, the number of Civil Service employees going on disability retirement is far greater than in the private sector. Between the ages of 30 and 50, Civil Service workers are 50 percent more likely to retire because of disability. Even at age 65, when private-sector disabilities crop up more often, a Civil Service worker is still 20 percent more likely to retire because of disability.

The Fringe Benefit Story Continues

Retirement pay, although the major fringe benefit employees receive, is only one part of the benefit package that costs the government more than the private sector. When it comes to other Federal job benefits, you see the same pattern of overspending; for example, excessive Federal costs for sick pay, vacation time, and injury claims, with no compensating gains in productivity. This has happened because the Federal workers' benefits are set in the political marketplace rather than by the healthy interaction of labor market supply and demand.

Federal health benefits cost nearly three-quarters of a billion dollars a year more than if they were based on the practices of the private sector. There are so many different Federal health plans that a Federal worker living in Washington, D.C., for example, has a smorgasbord of twenty-two alternative Federal health plans to choose from, while private-sector employees usually have a choice among two or three plans. This wide assortment of plans contributes to the government's increased health costs, which have risen by almost 25 percent each year from 1970 to 1981, about 40 percent more than in the private sector.

Government vacation benefits are more expensive, too. While the average private-sector worker gets five days after the first six months on the job, a Federal worker gets 6.5 days, or 30 percent more. After one year's service, the Federal worker gets 13 vacation days a year, versus the 10 days allowed in the private sector. After 15 years, the Federal worker gets 26 days per annum, compared to 19 days in private industry. It adds up to over $1.2 billion annually in extra costs.

Government sick leave is just as lopsided. Federal job regulations allow 13 days of sick leave to be accumulated or used each year. On average, 9 days are used and 4 accumulated. Nine sick days is excessive by private-sector standards, which show 5.5 days used on average in nonmanufacturing industries. Excessive sick-leave usage costs approximately $1.2 billion annually—yet the government has done little to control these costs.

Even Active Reserve Duty has its special privileges for Federal workers. Over 80 percent of the employees in the private sector who are also Army Reserve or Air National Guard members get pay differentials from their employers while they are on active duty, or are charged vacation time. In other words, if you work for a private-sector employer, while you are on active duty, your employer will pay you the difference between your regular pay and what the military pays you while on reserve duty. But Federal employees who are also Reserve members get their full regular pay, plus extra cash for active duty. This unearned bonus costs taxpayers $66 million over a three-year span.

Merely changing these benefits to match the best private-sector practices can save us billions. After all, since Federal workers are generally paid as well as, and in some cases better than, employees in private industry, why should their benefits be so much better?

The Joys of Overclassification

A 1982 Federal study found that about a third of the Federal jobs in the Washington, D.C., area are over-graded, and nearly half are incorrectly classified, with the wrong grade, occupation, or title. Throughout government, 14.3 percent of positions, or one out of every seven, are classified higher than they should be. For instance, a junior desk officer at the State Department could be making the salary of a senior desk officer while doing the work of a middle-level public affairs officer. How does a situation like this occur?

Government managers play a form of "classification gamesmanship." They do this since they feel that Civil Service regulations are too rigid to let them otherwise reward an employee's good work. So they give Federal employees unwarranted promotions. If they didn't stretch the rules, they'd be faced with situations such as the one the Navy faced in 1982: It was unable to fill 675 entry-level engineering positions because the pay system did not allow the Navy to offer competitive salaries.

Another factor is the annual "pay comparability" survey of white-collar Federal positions, which matches Federal and private-sector pay for similar positions. The survey looks at fifteen of the eighteen levels that cover 99 percent of the 1.4 million Federal white-collar employees. It is difficult (if not impossible) to place so many employees (in approximately 425 different occupations) into fifteen levels. So, some occupations are overpaid and some are underpaid. But the major fault is that this rigid survey just doesn't do the job of comparing Federal and private-sector pay for comparable positions.

The government's pay comparability surveys, meant to set Federal pay equal to that in private industry, are slanted toward the highest-paying private-industry jobs. And despite the fact that many Federal jobs are not too different from work in state and local government, or those at nonprofit enterprises, these institutions are excluded from the surveys. Also excluded are small- and medium-sized private-sector companies, which pay more modestly than the big corporations. The director of the Office of Personnel Management, one of the three people in charge of the survey, told Congress in 1983, "I can guarantee the survey is not an accurate survey." He said it looks at the wrong jobs and the wrong occupations in the wrong companies.

So, you have a system that does not allow managers to be flexible in meeting demand for some occupations, that is inaccurate in determining comparable pay levels in the private sector, and that overclassifies almost 200,000 employees, with one out of every four government white-collar employees (324,000) with the wrong grade, occupation, or title.

The salary irregularities of the government don't end there, however. Nearly three-quarters of Federal professional white-collar workers are now classified as upper management, whereas in private industry three-quarters of the workers are middle management or below. The Federal government thus has nearly three times the number of highly paid white-collar employees as are found in private industry. For instance, in the Department of Justice, lawyers do routine legal work that is effectively handled by paralegals in private industry, at half the cost. The Justice Department's ratio of attorneys to paralegals is 8 to 1, versus the private-sector ratio of 5 to 1. At the Department of Education, roughly a quarter of the employees are overclassified. Their average pay went up by 13.1 percent a year between 1979 and 1983. It rose by 17.3 percent in 1980 and 27.3 percent in 1981.

The Department of Energy has twice the number of supervisors per employee as the rest of the Federal government. There is one supervisor for every three employees, while the rest of the Federal government has one supervisor for every seven subordinates. Just bringing the Energy Department into line with the rest of government would cut 120 unneeded management positions, saving taxpayers $19 million over three years.

Federal blue-collar workers also come off better than their private-sector counterparts. They generally make 8 percent more per year than blue-collar workers in private industry. This occurs because of the distortions resulting from the use of a five-level wage scale for Federal blue-collar workers. Only the two lowest levels are comparable to private-industry pay. The grades beyond the first two give blue-collar workers a premium wage compared to their counterparts in private business. Since 85 percent of government blue-collar workers are in levels 3, 4, and 5, most blue-collar employees are getting higher-than-comparable wages.

But at the top of the government pyramid, where experience and continuity are most needed, the salaries are uncompetitively low. Salaries for the Senior Executive Service are set at a maximum of about $70,000 a year. Some lawyers barely out of law school make more than that these days. These relatively low salaries can't come close to private-sector pay for the best managerial talent. Therefore, at the upper levels of government there is a revolving door through which talented management comes and goes. The average tenure of political appointees in Federal agencies is only eighteen months. Over the past ten years, there have been nine Administrators, ten Deputy Administrators, and fourteen Procurement Commissioners at the General Services Administration.

Public Productivity

We've heard much about productivity over the last few years—with good reason, for productivity is what creates wealth. Rising output per unit of input has contributed to the long-term rise in American incomes over the decades. We're richer because our output per unit of input increased. We became more efficient. We did this first by moving off inefficient family farms into factories, where machines helped us do more work. Lately, computers and robots are increasing productivity.

In business, the rewards of increased productivity show up as higher profits, and increased wages for the most productive workers. The government, of course, has no bottom line as such, because it doesn't make a profit. It can't possibly fail financially. A Civil Service worker who conscientiously does his job more efficiently is not likely to see his initiative rewarded in his paycheck or in any other way. And if you were in his shoes, would you try very hard to be so efficient?

Look at it from a Federal manager's point of view: He's paid based on the number of employees he supervises and the rank of those employees. The more workers he supervises, and the higher their grades, the more pay he receives. He isn't rewarded for being an effective manager; that hardly counts in the Federal government. He's not paid for cost control, or efficiency, or for effectiveness. He's rewarded only for running a big bureaucratic empire, and the bigger the better as far as his paycheck is concerned. There's no incentive to be productive. There's an overwhelming incentive for him to build an ever-bigger castle of paperwork, seniority, and encrusted regulatory rigidity.

So we end up with myriad situations such as that at the Department of Health and Human Services, where a single response to correspondence needing the signature of the Secretary involves from 55 to 60 people and takes forty-seven days to finish. The Veterans Administration requires twenty days. Even the biggest corporation can do the job in about five days. A staff study for Congress noted that "if the overall Federal productivity could be increased by 10 percent, personnel costs could be reduced by more than $8 billion per year without a cutback in services."

We badly need to reform the whole government personnel

system, so that pay, retirement, and the other benefits match the best of the private sector, but are not greater. We also need to rearrange the system so Federal employees have ample incentive to work productively and spend our tax dollars wisely. In doing this, we could save $91 billion over three years.

Chapter 6

How to Cut $100 Billion from Defense

The $436 Hammer

A man in California was assessed $2,400 in back taxes by the Internal Revenue Service. So he decided to send the IRS six hammers in lieu of the cash. He informed the IRS that after reading about what the government pays for them, he figured he should pay his debts in hammers. "If those smart fellows in the Pentagon are paying $436 per hammer," he wrote, "no doubt you clever gentlemen of the IRS will accept these hammers at the same value" (in which case the six hammers more than covered the $2,400 owed). Actually, the man would have saved postage by mailing the IRS twenty-six three-penny screws, for which the Defense Department has been paying $91.

How did the government manage to pay $436 for a hammer that could be purchased in a neighborhood hardware store for $7?

The Navy, the purchaser of the hammer, provided the following explanation. Added to the basic $7 cost of the hammer was:

- $41 to pay general overhead costs for the engineering staff involved in mapping out the hammer problem. This included 12 minutes in secretarial time preparing the hammer purchase order, 26 minutes of management time

88

spent on the hammer purchase, and 2 hours and 36 minutes the engineers spent on determining the hammer's specifications.

- $93 for the 18 minutes it took for "mechanical subassembly" of the hammer, 4 hours for engineers to map out the hammer assembly process, 90 minutes spent by managers overseeing the hammer manufacturing process, 60 minutes for a project engineer to ensure the hammer was properly assembled, 54 minutes spent by quality-control engineers examining the hammer to ensure it did not have any defects, and 7 hours and 48 minutes devoted to other support activities involved in assembling the hammer.
- $102 went toward "manufacturing overhead."
- $37 for the 60 minutes the "spares repair department" spent gearing up for either repairing or finding parts should the hammer ever break.
- $2 for "material handling overhead" representing the payroll costs for the people to wrap the hammer and send it out.
- $1 for wrapping paper and a box.

This brought the subtotal of costs for the hammer to $283.

This figure was increased by $90, representing the defense contractor's general administrative costs, and another $56 was added in a finder's fee for locating the specific hammer that fitted the Navy's needs.

Another $7 was added as the "capital cost of money" for the hammer purchase.

A Navy spokesman explained that large defense contractors are permitted to charge off general costs against all contracted items, and that in the case of relatively inexpensive items these costs *may* appear disproportionately large. I have to agree; $436 for a $7 hammer does appear to be a "disproportionately large" price to pay.

The Defense Department is an easy target, but most of the self-styled "marksmen," especially in Congress, are likely as not to wind up shooting themselves in the foot. That is, critics are quick to call for cuts in crucial defense projects they don't like for political reasons. But they fight with all their might to preserve the most outrageous instances of Pentagon inefficiency and boondoggle if it has any bearing on a Congressman's home district, or if it affects any of his constituents, or if it raises the faintest protest from the Congressman's pet branch of the service.

The military isn't without guilt in this game. Military lobbyists play on Congressional loyalties in trying to get new military programs started or to get existing programs expanded or continued. Almost two-thirds of all Congressional districts either contain or are next to some military facility. This proximity results in what's called "reciprocal pork barrel" in Washington. An obsolete military facility is maintained in one district and, in return, the Representative of that district will vote to continue funding for a weapons system that even the military may no longer want or support.

Out of 4,000 Defense Department installations in America, only 312 are considered significant and necessary. The rest are support facilities—storage depots, for example—with fewer than 150 employees each. They survive, eating up taxpayer dollars, because Congress has passed laws to make closing unnecessary facilities a time-consuming, almost impossible chore. Congress seems to look on the Pentagon as its own personal pork barrel.

With all the proposals from Congress calling for reduced defense spending, the truth is that Congress will put more than $6 billion in the 1985 budget that was not requested by the Defense Department. How do you explain this paradox? Additions to the military budget channel money into the home districts of Congressmen who sponsor them, producing jobs and spending that result in votes. These additions are not necessitated by military requirements, although they are sold

90

on this aspect; how else could the spending be justified?

To reduce the military budget, Congress will cut spending on essential items to accommodate its own pet projects. Operational spending is cut first, followed by ammunition and wartime supplies. Funds are moved in and out of programs until programs with little or no political constituency are cut in lieu of projects with more favored backing.

The $126-Billion Grab Bag

There's one overwhelming reason why Congress so often intervenes in the management of the Defense Department. In the entire Federal budget, $210.5 billion is called "controllable outlays" or "discretionary spending," as they say in Washington. It's that part of the budget that is easiest for Congress to manipulate. (The rest of the budget is "uncontrollable," Congress will have you believe, because it involves expenditures mandated by specific laws and by prior years' contracts and obligations.) Of the $210.5 billion in discretionary spending, $126.2 billion, 60 percent of the total, is Defense Department money.

The Congressmen who prevent obsolete military bases from being closed are often the same ones who complain most loudly about high defense costs. However, despite evidence of great waste in military spending, the trend of defense costs as a percentage of the Gross National Product (GNP) has been downward. In the Eisenhower years, defense spending was 11.2 percent of GNP, and in the Kennedy-Johnson years, 9.0 percent of GNP. By the 1970s it had dropped to 5.9 percent of GNP, and in 1983 it was still at a relatively low 6.5 percent of GNP. Between 1971 and 1983, the Soviet Union spent $2.0 trillion for defense, versus our $1.5 trillion—or one-third more than the U.S.

None of us would seriously suggest the weakening of our defense in the name of budget-cutting. We do, however, want a national defense that is efficient, in which limited resources—our tax dollars—are put where they'll do the most good, get "the most bang for the buck."

A bit of history: The Office of the Secretary of Defense was created by the National Security Act of 1947. It was intended to unify the armed forces. During the Second World War, it was found that the separate War and Navy departments were not coordinating their efforts and were thus performing at less than optimal efficiency. President Harry Truman warned in 1945 that "One of the lessons which has most clearly come from the costly and dangerous experience [the Second World War] is that there must be unified direction of land, sea and air forces at home, as well as in all other parts of the world where our Armed Forces are serving. We did not have that kind of direction when we were attacked four years ago—and we certainly paid a high price for not having it." Harry Truman knew up close whereof he spoke. And unfortunately, some thirty-seven years later, this unification hasn't really happened, and this has been, and continues to be, costly.

As I noted earlier, one consequence of the lack of coordination between the services is that weapons programs, once started, are rarely curtailed even if developments suggest that those programs are no longer necessary. The military managers of a program fight to keep it going at all costs. Members of Congress, local communities, and local businessmen jealously protect the flow of money spent on "their" military bases and "their" weapons programs, regardless of the practicality, necessity, or cost-effectiveness of those bases and programs.

Special benefit provisions put in place when military pay was lower than private-sector pay are maintained even though military pay has been greatly increased and is fully comparable to salaries in the private sector.

For example, in 1981 the Navy and Marine Corps started giving out cash bonuses to keep fliers from retiring. But as much as $82 million out of the entire $103 million provided for these bonuses has been misused. Some $25 million was given out to Marine Corps and Navy pilots who are in grades in which there are actually surpluses of fliers. Twenty-eight million dollars was given to Navy pilots who are too old to fly anyway. Twenty-nine million dollars was divided up among Naval Flight Officers, of whom there are no shortages and with whom there are no recruiting problems.

Then, beyond all specific examples of waste and inefficiency is the general expectation by the Army, Navy, and Air Force that their historic roles and shares of the military budget will always be maintained. Each service must have its own bases, hospitals, housing and garbage collection services, canteens and officers' clubs. These branches of the service resist centralization and coordination of their activities under the Secretary of Defense, thereby limiting their ability to adapt to meet the challenge of new world circumstances.

Sergeant Bilko, Where Are You?

The Defense Department manages two million military personnel and almost one million civilian workers—scattered in 5,600 installations around the world. The Pentagon thus employs about two-thirds of all Federal employees. If you add in the three million defense contract employees, the Defense Department, directly or indirectly, employs about 5 percent of the U.S. labor force.

The economics are mind-boggling, and the sheer size of the bureaucracy explains the pervasive waste and inefficiency. The Defense Department spends a quarter of all Federal outlays. That accounted for 6.5 percent of the entire U.S. Gross National Product in 1983. Just the $60 billion budgeted by the Defense Department for major weapons systems represents about 8 percent of the whole Federal budget.

The political cycle almost assures a complete change of top management at the Defense Department every few years. In fact, the average Secretary of Defense only stays on the job for twenty-six months. Then, routine military transfers pull officers out of the Pentagon after three years of service. And as we have seen in chapter 5, perverse military and Civil Service retirement policies provide incentives for successful managers to retire just when their experience brings them to the peak of productivity.

The worst part of this whole turnover problem is the way our laws put a tight cap on top managerial salaries, while salaries at lower levels are higher than they need to be in comparison to private-sector standards. I'm a firm believer in paying for what you get, but the Pentagon seems to take pride in paying for what it doesn't get, and in not paying for what it ought to get, thanks to Congress through its politically motivated and shortsighted Federal pay legislation. (Congressional salaries are set in conjunction with the top pay levels for civilian and military Executive Branch personnel. Congressional increases in salary are politically sensitive, and this has had the impact of restricting pay increases throughout the highest levels of government.) In any case, the salaries at the top of the Pentagon are simply not high enough to keep the best top management, except for those relatively few who are driven by psychological rewards. But if they are so driven, they'll likely crash into a brick wall at the Defense Department. Frustration over not being able to make the right things happen drives a lot of good people to leave the Pentagon after brief careers. They just get fed up.

If Only the Missiles Went as Fast as Their Costs

Cost estimates for twenty-five major weapons systems

94

started between 1971 and 1978 have increased 223 percent. Inflation is partly to blame, as the projects drag on year after year, delay after bureaucratic delay. But another important reason they occur is because defense contractors know that if they vastly underbid on a job, they can subsequently recover their costs, and the Pentagon has no choice but to pay up.

The Pentagon, in fact, encourages underbidding on major weapons systems. The Office of Management and Budget estimated that the fourteen major new weapons systems for which funds were requested in 1983 and 1984 would bring the military's total weapons systems costs to 2.3 times the funds likely to be available. Obviously not all the weapons systems proposed and in progress can be completed as scheduled. However, rather than establishing spending priorities, the military (with the support, and often the insistence, of Congress) continues to develop and procure all weapons systems at a slower, stretched-out rate. Program stretch-out inevitably results in higher costs, but once a weapons system is underway, it develops its own constituency and is almost impossible to discontinue—whether needed or not. The "trigger" to this wasteful process is the low initial cost estimate submitted by defense contractors.

Sometimes the contractors underbid by underestimating the difficulty of a project. This is not much different than the local garage mechanic saying, "Oh, it'll only cost you about a hundred dollars to fix the transmission. No problem, we'll fix it right up." But when you go to pick up your car (two weeks later), the bill says $400. What can you do? If you want your car, you pay the bill, meditate on the injustices of life, and have your martini an hour early that evening.

The Pentagon invites these cost overruns by using "cost plus" contracts whereby a contractor recovers his costs, plus a profit. So why should a defense contractor be particularly concerned about his costs? Uncle Sam is paying. Whether he buys a 3-cent screw or an identical $91 screw, it doesn't come out of his pocket anyway. Also, the Defense Department always wants the latest technology included in its weapons. Often the latest technology just isn't ready for demanding military applications, and trying to include it only drags out the construction time and raises costs still further. Contractors who underbid on defense contracts anticipate the military's "change orders," since this provides the opportunity to offset their low initial bid. A few specific examples may be useful.

The Navy's Harpoon missile was stretched out from six years to ten years in production, increasing the original cost from $2.6 billion to $3.5 billion. And the Navy was only able to hold down costs to that $3.5-billion figure by deciding to buy 2,585 of the Harpoon missiles instead of the originally planned 2,870. The Navy LAMPS MK III was stretched out from a four-year to a nine-year delivery schedule, pushing the cost of the program from $4.3 billion up to nearly $7 billion.

Another reason for the high cost of Pentagon weapons is the fact that they are bought usually on yearly contracts. Contracts for the purchase of a weapons system depend on annual appropriations from Congress. Although a one-year supply of weapons is ordered, the manufacturer has to gear up production and expend funds for capital equipment and personnel that may not be requested beyond the initial year. Multiyear contracting would reduce the inefficiency and costliness of having contractors rev up the production line at large start-up costs, which are passed on to the military.

Last year, the Navy wanted to use multiyear contracts, since it estimated that it could save $208 million on production of the MK-45 gun, $135 million on F-14 aircraft, $16 million on the MK-48 torpedo, and so on. Roughly a total of $630 million a year could be saved. But Congress rejected the Navy's request. Congressmen view multiyear contracts as a limitation on their power to cancel military weapons programs or to vote in new ones every year.

The Air Force could save $3.5 billion if it were allowed to use multiyear contracting for weapons like the F-16 fighter ($257 million), the GPS navigational satellite ($243 million), the KC-10 wide-body transport ($658 million), plus a long list of other weapons systems.

When a new missile or helicopter is on the drawing boards, private companies compete fiercely to get the contract. Newspapers run daily accounts of whether Lockheed or Boeing is about to win the prize. The battling is bloody. And for good reason, from the defense contractor's point of view. Because once he's in, he's in for the long haul—twenty years or more. He becomes the government's monopoly supplier of the weapons system that was so fiercely fought over. After the ink is dry on the contract, the champagne chilled, and the toasts delivered, there will be no arguments.

Of course, the main thing that monopolies do is raise prices. Defense contractor monopolies are no different.

So that after a company has won a contract to develop and produce, say, a missile system, it can go to work on raising prices. In private business, a customer would refuse to accept unjustified price increases and would go to alternative producers. But the government, painted into a corner by its procurement procedures, doesn't have that option. The government generally accepts the higher prices. The average final cost of military weapons systems is in the range of 30 to 50 percent higher than the original agreed-upon price.

Is this not a case of business immorality, of business ripping off the government? It's a complicated question. Business's first loyalty is to the income statement. Business wants to make a profit, as long as it is neither illegal nor harmful. And there's the Defense Department, giving out monopolies like candy. Should a company refuse to participate because existing Defense Department procurement procedures waste taxpayer money? If you disagree with the way the government gives out student loans, does that mean you're not going to apply for one when your children reach college age? The fact that you or a company doesn't partake of the largess doesn't change government policy one iota. The individual consequences differ in the two cases, however. If you won't take out an unneeded student loan, you have made a sacrifice for moral reasons, and you are to be congratulated for such courage. Now if a company refused to seek a defense contract because it would constitute an unfair monopoly, the stockholders would quite legitimately feel cheated and question the capability of the company's management. The job of business is not to look after the government's morality, but to make a return on the stockholders' investment.

Jack McVickers, director of productivity improvement at Martin Marietta, said, "While our stockholders may all be very patriotic individuals, they do not allow us to invest their money in capacity or inventory that sits idle [waiting for a weapons program to be funded]. . . . Nor do they allow us to purchase labor-saving machinery when the government gets to keep all of the savings. They will not put their money at risk on a project that promises a 15 percent return when they are guaranteed a higher return elsewhere with little or no risk [a defense contract, for instance]. Such motivation is the basis of our free enterprise system and we do not apologize for it."

The real immorality is in the Defense Department giving out these licenses to steal from the taxpayers. An obvious solution is for the Pentagon to award more than one contract for the same item, so that while one company makes half the number of missiles required, a competitor would make the rest. Not only would that cut costs, as the two compete with each other in price, but with two or more parallel producers of a weapons system, we're sure to have a ready supply of new weapons in case of a major mobilization.

The Navy has tried to go part of the way toward this "dual-sourcing" in one program, its Airborne Self-Protection Jammer. It's a device to interfere with enemy radar. What the

Navy did was to set two teams of two contractors against each other in battle for the Jammer development contract. The two contractors on the winning team will then be pitted against each other for the awarding of the actual production contract.

The Air Force tried "dual-sourcing" for its Advanced Medium-Range Air-to-Air Missile, with excellent savings, plus the missiles were delivered on time, a rare occurrence. Indeed, a dozen different studies done for the Air Force between 1965 and 1979 claim savings from 15 to 52 percent.

Now about those $91 screws and $436 hammers: The Air Force keeps 900,000 spare parts in stock, worth more than $17 billion. The Navy keeps 80,000 ship and plane parts in inventory on a single carrier, worth $125 million. The Air Force, for example, purchases less than 25 percent of replenishment spare parts directly.

The prime contractors mark up the prices of spare parts from subcontractors. It's the old monopoly situation again. And as in the case of the $436 hammer, we have large overhead costs allocated to inexpensive spare parts. Thus we get 60-cent light bulbs for $511, and $100 each for aircraft simulator parts that can be had down at the hardware store for a quarter. A Minuteman II missile screw cost the Pentagon $1.09 last year. This year's price for the same screw: $36.77 each. This excess can add up, because the services purchase over $22 billion a year in spare parts for weapons systems and other equipment.

The Alaskan Transfer

Aside from the savings available from more efficient purchasing of major weapons systems and spare parts, the Pentagon has opportunities to realize gains by better "housekeeping." A major saving is to be had by bringing pay and benefits back in line with the private sector, as we saw in chapter 5. However, there is much more to be done. For example:

A study shows 71 percent of all household goods shipments arranged by the Pentagon to Alaska are either reported as lost or damaged in transit.

Further, restrictive language in some obscure appropriations bill prohibits the military from offering competitive bids on household moves to Alaska and Hawaii, with the result that these moving costs are more than a fifth higher than they ought to be. Just by using competitive bidding the Pentagon could save $63 million over three years, and a lot of broken furniture besides.

The Defense Department tries to do everything in-house. The Pentagon has nearly 12,000 people doing the laundry, cleaning offices, serving food in military cafeterias, fire fighting, and collecting the garbage. If the Pentagon contracted out this kind of work, as private industry and many local governments do, it could save us $70 million a year.

The Air Force has attempted to contract out some of its work, and since 1965 it has been able to convert some 58,000 military positions to civilian jobs. The Air Force had planned to convert 6,000 more jobs. But Congress imposed limits making it possible to convert only 1,800 of these positions. And after Congress was informed that the Air Force had successfully contracted out some thirty-four functions, saving $108 million, it forbade any more contracting out.

The Defense Department used 7.5 billion gallons of petroleum in fiscal 1981, which is 80 percent of all Federal usage (and 2 percent of the entire U.S. demand). But while the government exhorts private citizens to economize, the government itself continues to waste fuel in massive quantities. The Pentagon could save more than a billion dollars over three years in fuel costs just by doing what the airlines do when their planes take off and land. It's called thrust/power management, meaning cutting power on takeoff, trimming back engine speed to the proper specifications, and otherwise taking care not to waste fuel.

The military commissaries (see chapter 9) were set up to serve soldiers in isolated frontier posts, but now there are 238 of them in the U.S., including six in an "outpost" such as Washington, D.C., five in San Francisco and San Antonio, four in Norfolk and San Diego, and so on. These commissaries, which merely duplicate private grocery markets, but without the profit motive, cost taxpayers nearly a billion dollars a year.

The Army Corps of Engineers leased the International Tower Building at Baltimore-Washington Airport on an "as-is" basis and couldn't move in for fifteen months. But the Corps still paid rent on the unusable space, amounting to $600,000. Speaking of wasting space, the average occupancy rate in military hospitals in 1981 was 46 percent, compared to 80 percent in private hospitals. And yet, the government spent $550 million to reimburse private hospitals for the care of military personnel.

The cost of issuing an Army payroll check is $4.20 each. That is more than four times the private-sector average and creates a $40-million-a-year inefficiency.

The Navy didn't bother to charge some $4.3 million in required fees for military sales to a foreign country—a savings to the foreign country with the taxpayers making up the difference. There was no strategic or tactical justification, only sloppy bookkeeping.

By correcting the major inefficiencies, we can save $120 billion over three years. That figure does not include the savings we would realize by making military pay and benefits comparable to those in the best private-sector plans, as discussed in chapter 5.

Billions can be saved by using multiyear defense contracts, "dual-sourcing," and the general good management techniques detailed in our reports. Another $7.3 billion can be saved if we simply standardize common hardware components. A $6-billion savings would come from improving the Pentagon's inventory systems and updating the computers that keep track of supplies and spare parts.

Closing or realigning useless military bases would save $2.7 billion. Prioritizing weapons programs to be consistent with available funding would save $1.5 billion. Consolidating maintenance depots would save $589 million, and buying fuel by competitive bid would save $513 million. This is only a rough sample of the many small changes we recommend.

By making our national defense efficient, we can eliminate at least $100 billion in military waste over three years. This will come without costing us a single important weapons program, without dismantling any of our defenses, and without forgoing new weapons systems.

Chapter 7

Thirty Cents on the Dollar

Get Off My Back

A veteran returning from Korea went to college on the GI bill; bought his house with an FHA loan; saw his kids born in a VA hospital; started a business with an SBA loan; got electricity from TVA and, later, water from an EPA project. His parents retired to a farm on Social Security, got electricity from the Rural Electrification Administration (REA), and soil testing from the Department of Agriculture. When his father became ill, the family was saved from financial ruin by Medicare and his life was saved with a drug developed through the National Institutes of Health (NIH). His kids took part in the school lunch program, learned physics from teachers trained in National Science Foundation (NSF) programs and went through college with guaranteed student loans. He drove to work on the Interstate and moored his boat in a channel dredged by Army engineers. When floods hit, he took Amtrak to Washington to apply for disaster relief, and spent some time in the Smithsonian museums. Then one day he wrote his Congressman an angry letter asking the government to get off his back. He angrily declared that he resented paying taxes for all those programs created for other people.

Ironically, while we enjoy taking advantage of the benefits government offers us, we don't like paying for them. What, then, is the moral? Well, there are actually two morals, and the one you pick generally reflects your political inclination.

103

If you think that only government can solve the problems that confront us, then you're likely to reply that the man in our story should gratefully pay his taxes and continue taking advantage of the myriad programs available to him. If, however, you're not an admirer of Big Government and the welfare state, you would say that the man in the story has to be willing to sacrifice some of his government benefits if he wants to lower his taxes.

Somebody has to pay for the things government provides. The government doesn't have any money. It can't even cover current spending levels with taxes, so how can anyone advocate even greater spending? The problem is for people to figure out what they truly think government needs to provide, as opposed to those things that it would be nice to have—the true obligations of our government to *all* its citizens rather than the handouts granted the fortunate few. To improve the financial position of people, the easiest approach is simply to forcibly take money from the wealthy and hand it to the poor, much like Robin Hood—except we now call it redistribution of income. The real-life version, as practiced by our government, has become an absurd parody of the theory. In real life, what we're doing is confiscating money not from the rich but from middle- and lower-income working people, because that's where the money is—as we have mentioned, 90 percent of all taxable income is from the first $35,000 of everyone's pretax annual income. Then, the government "redistributes" the money, but most of it is "redistributed" back to middle-income people, not to poor people, and much of the rest is "mistargeted." For instance, one dollar in ten that goes for food stamp benefits is in error—either the amount is wrong or the person is not eligible. That alone amounts to $1 billion—the equivalent of the income taxes paid by 450,000 median-income families. And in 1982, food stamps were handed out to 413,000 families earning more than $15,000 a year, along with 204,000 households earning over $20,000 a year. Indeed, more than a quarter of all households getting food stamps had cash incomes above the poverty level. And the school lunch program even subsidizes lunches for the children of parents making over $100,000 a year. Are these the truly needy people that our tax dollars are supposed to help? How many American families are aware of how their tax dollars are being wasted by their elected representatives?

Our welfare system has moved beyond—well beyond—the point of providing a "social safety net." It now provides disincentives to those who might otherwise seek gainful employment and contributes to the formation of a permanent underclass based on welfare dependence. This is the inescapable consequence of increasing welfare benefits to the point where they are competitive with the salaries of lower-, and even middle-, income families.

In New York State, for example, in 1981 an hourly wage of $4.87 would have to be earned in order to equal the welfare benefits available—hourly earnings one and one half times the minimum wage. Who's going to work in McDonald's at $3.35 an hour when they can "earn" $4.87 an hour on welfare?

And our welfare system doesn't cure poverty, it only combats the symptoms. Work cures poverty; welfare perpetuates it.

The alternative, and the only real way to improve the financial and general condition of individuals and of society, is by encouraging the creation of new jobs and by eliminating disincentives to work. By allowing individual effort to be rewarded, we provide the incentive for future improvements in productivity and the opportunity to increase wealth. Most people will choose to exercise their talent and ingenuity to maximize their well-being. However, if the rewards of risk taking and hard work are taxed away, who's going to start new businesses, and if you can do as well or better by not working, who's going to fill the jobs created by those new businesses anyway?

105

This spirit of entrepreneurship benefits not only the individual but the community, rich and poor alike. To start an enterprise, you have to commit capital, saved or borrowed, and you have to hire people. People need jobs, and most new jobs in this country come from small new companies. New companies are the source of 80 percent of new jobs in the country and 60 percent of the U.S. workforce are employed by small businesses.

This idea of reducing the burden of taxes, and lessening the intrusion of government in our day-to-day lives, is as American as apple pie. Our country grew and prospered because men and women could come here from all over the world and freely try to work for their own success. Many failed, but more succeeded. Their success has made our country the envy of the world. Our experience proves the vast superiority of the free enterprise system.

The Nanny State

Let's compare it with the welfare-state mentality of those legions who see the government as the national nanny, the parent-figure there to supply baby with all his wants, cradle-to-grave. In contrast to the spirit of risk-taking entrepreneurship, welfare-state aficionados crave security. They want a guaranteed job at a guaranteed pay. In the welfare state, risk taking and productivity become alien concepts. Actually, many would prefer to be paid for doing nothing, and sometimes, in some countries, they can pull it off. Policies that move us toward a welfare state are often justified on the basis of the common good, yet, in analyzing these policies, we find their basis in selfishness rather than selflessness.

You needn't go to Moscow to find this attitude. It's common in any of the welfare states of Western Europe. It is also highly touted in some of our universities, and you can even find the spirit of the welfare state in the halls of the Washington bureaucracy. There's a certain amount of it in large corporations. You find it wherever entrenched protection and security is the watchword, where innovators are feared and hated.

The welfare protectionist mentality has a debilitating effect on people. As French critics have eloquently demonstrated, the French welfare state has become a society of mistrust. Everyone fights over how to divide up the economic pie, with little thought to making a bigger pie. Worker is pitted against employer, city dweller against farmer, customer against seller in a never-ending series of conflicts over who gets to be protected the most.

Are we heading that miserable way? We are already on the road to welfare socialism. We walk along this road by accommodating those who crave the protective security of government patronage. This patronage is in the form of government "transfer payments." Transfer payments are funds that have been taken from some citizens (through taxes) and transferred into the hands of other citizens. In many cases, it winds up back in taxpayers' pockets. It is the official term for income redistribution.

Since 1962, the amount of "transfer payments" handed out by the U.S. Government has risen two and a half times as fast as government spending in all other areas. In 1950 there were 4.2 wage-earners for every transfer payment recipient; in 1980, there were 1.6 wage-earners for each transfer payment recipient. These subsidies, to the elderly, to those counted as poor, and to businesses, were less than half of all Federal outlays in 1962. Now they are almost two-thirds of outlays. That is, two-thirds of everything the government does. It now equals $462 billion a year. Exactly who gets all the income transfers?

107

In 1982 a quarter of total budget outlays of $728 billion—some $174 billion—went to the elderly. Other individual recipients received $97 billion. This was spent primarily on veterans: $15 billion; military personnel, retirees and their dependents: $19 billion; Social Security benefits to survivors and dependents: $15 billion; and the disabled: $18 billion. State and local governments, along with nonprofit groups, got more than $62 billion. The poor, and the alleged poor, got $62 billion in means-tested benefits. The unemployed got $24 billion. (In 1982, the average cash family income in the United States was $26,799. The average income with one or more family members unemployed was $19,316. Even after six months of unemployment, family income remained at $18,059.) Farmers got $14.3 billion. Businesses got $7.8 billion. A variety of other transfer payments amounted to $21 billion. As a percentage of our Gross National Product, transfer payments increased to 12.2 percent in 1982, 3.2 times the 3.8 percent level of 1952.

The Federal government runs 400 programs to give subsidies to individuals, with fifteen program categories accounting for 97 percent of all transfers to individuals. These include Social Security; Medicare; Unemployment Insurance and Benefits; Veterans' Major Benefits; Federal Disability Insurance; Medicaid; Food and Nutrition Programs; Military Retirement Pay; Civil Service Retirement and Disability; Low Income Housing Programs; Aid for Families with Dependent Children (AFDC); Supplemental Security Income (SSI); Railroad Retirement; Military Benefits; and Guaranteed Student Loans. From 1970 to 1980, payments to individuals increased 1.5 times as fast as GNP and 2.1 times as fast as the average hourly wage in private industry. You can't get something from nothing, and the only way some people can get larger shares of our economic pie is for others to get less. Is it fair for those who made the pie in the first place to get the smaller slice? How long do you think they'll go on making pies?

Why Hasn't Poverty Gone Away?

Throughout most of our country's history, welfare has been a matter of individual conscience with responsibility almost exclusively assumed by local governments and private charities. Rather than providing an alternative life-style for recipients, welfare was intended to meet the short-term needs of people in trouble. Both those who received it and those who paid for it understood that the objective was to increase self-reliance and decrease dependency as quickly as possible. And, of great importance, those responsible for administering welfare programs were the friends and neighbors of both donors and recipients. This was, however, to change.

In the mid-1960s, President Lyndon Johnson sounded the clarion for a War on Poverty. A "war" he thought we could wage and win since America was the most affluent society on earth. Federal bureaucrats were eager to engage the enemy. However, the welfare bureaucrat created by this system was far removed from the local pressures experienced by his predecessors. Reducing dependency was most definitely not in his best interest. He could afford to be generous since his spending was not limited by affordability. Yet, since then, something very curious has happened. The poverty rate initially went down, but in recent years it has increased.

This cannot be blamed on recessions, which came and went without having much effect on the percentage of hard-core poor. It also contradicts the usual political response—that it was somehow the fault of "uncompassionate" government—because antipoverty spending has steadily increased under both Republican and Democratic administrations. In fact the period of greatest growth in social spending was in the 1970s, when such champions of unrestrained free enterprise as Richard M. Nixon were at the helm. And now we have 22 million Medicaid recipients (more people received Medicaid in 1980 than received aid from all social programs in

1950), 20 million food stamp recipients, 4 million Supplemental Security Income recipients, and 11 million recipients of Aid to Families with Dependent Children (welfare).

Some 63.4 percent of the 1982 total Federal government outlays represented money targeted at wiping out poverty, providing retirement benefits, and assisting farmers and businessmen with direct aid, credit, preferential tax treatment, or some combination of the three.

Now since the Federal government is spending such a large proportion of its resources on these social programs, one might ask why it is that the poverty rate has been getting worse. The government first began measuring poverty in the early 1960s, when the U.S. had reached rather comfortable affluence. But in 1959, the poverty statistics said we had 22 percent of the population who were poor. That amounted to almost 40 million Americans, one out of every five. The solid economic growth and the Great Society programs of the 1960s sent the American poverty rate plummeting to a low of 11.1 percent in 1973. Throughout the rest of the 1970s, it hung in the area of 11 percent to 12 percent. But then the poverty rate increased again, and hit 15 percent in 1982. How did the poverty rate increase even though Federal government transfer payments quintupled in real dollars between 1959 and 1982; and even though the government's "means-tested" programs (providing aid when income falls below some predetermined level) aimed specifically at the poor multiplied more than sixfold?

Part of the answer becomes apparent when you analyze poverty statistics. The government defines poverty in terms of cash income only, whether it be pay for work or other earnings, Social Security retirement benefits, or cash aid to the poor. Yet a substantial portion of all transfer payments are in noncash form. And the majority of means-tested programs, including in-kind medical benefits, housing assistance, food stamps, and school lunches, are now in noncash form. Indeed, between 1959 and 1983, noncash payments soared 43.4 times for means-tested programs and 82.2 times overall. By 1983 noncash income transfers amounted to about 30 percent of all transfer payments—72 percent of benefits under means-tested programs.

If we add all those noncash transfers into the poverty statistics, does it change our conclusions about the poor in America? If a poor person gets $250 a month as a rent subsidy, how is that different from providing $250 in cash? If we did count noncash transfers along with cash transfers and other forms of income, we'd find that the 1982 poverty rate of 15 percent would instead be 9.6 percent. That's a rather huge drop. A 15 percent poverty rate represents roughly 34 million Americans. A 9.6 percent rate comes to about 22 million people. The additional "poverty" created by bad statistics represents 12 million people.

Even if we added in noncash transfers, the poverty figures still might exaggerate the rate of real poverty. The household surveys used each year by the Census Bureau to gauge poverty are based on voluntary responses. Studies by the Office of Management and Budget (OMB) indicate that the benefits received are underreported. People forget to mention the aid they're getting, perhaps for fear of losing it. So OMB estimates that about 19 percent of all benefits are underreported, and 33 percent of all means-tested benefits are underreported. That could add up to as much as $62 billion in total benefits that are left out of the poverty statistics.

Beyond the Census Survey underreporting, there are numerous programs that aren't included. The surveys cover only the major means-tested programs such as Food Stamps and Medicaid. They exclude more than sixty other programs that give out over $40 billion on the basis of income eligibility tests. Small change—equivalent to the annual taxes of more than 18 million median-income American families.

The inescapable conclusion is that, despite the billions

spent on Federal income transfers, adequate information doesn't exist to determine how many recipients are getting sufficient benefits or, conversely, how much in benefits is being paid to those who don't need them. In fact, the Federal government doesn't have a way to find out the amount of all the subsidies any given person receives. Major policy decisions concerning the poor are therefore being made on the basis of surveys that significantly underreport income and benefits and exclude many other antipoverty benefits.

In the absence of good information and adequate controls, it's not surprising that, between 1980 and 1982, the Social Security Administration made $14.6 billion in erroneous payments, and that food stamp overpayments totalled $1 billion in 1981, and that estimated overpayments for fiscal 1981 in the Supplemental Security Income program totaled more than $400 million—an average overpayment of $105 per recipient.

But the real shocker is that only 30 cents of each antipoverty dollar actually goes to help the poor and reduce poverty. The other 70 cents goes to the nonpoor and for the administration of the programs. In 1982, for example, we spent $124 billion to reduce poverty, yet those expenditures reduced poverty by only $37 billion, or 30 percent of the total expenditures. After spending the $124 billion in means-tested programs to help the poor rise above the aggregate $50 billion poverty gap, there is still a $13 billion poverty gap remaining. In theory, the $124 billion should have been enough not merely to bring poor households up to the poverty level, but also to bring these and all other households up to 125 percent of the poverty level, and still have $48 billion left over for other purposes, such as reducing the deficit.

Why, then, are our vast antipoverty expenditures so badly missing the mark? One reason is that only one-third of the seventy-two Federal antipoverty programs have income eligibility tests that relate to the official poverty line. Even those programs establish eligibility limits that are above the poverty line. You don't have to be poor (as defined by the government) to participate in antipoverty programs.

The remaining two-thirds of the Federal antipoverty programs establish eligibility based on state or regional median-income statistics. Some forty-two states collect quarterly wage information from employers. It is the best available source of information about income levels, but yet it does not include money earned from Federal government work, military service, or self-employment. Social Security data does include that information, but Congress allows the Social Security figures to be used only by the Food Stamp and AFDC programs, and then only after the data is twenty months old. Whether using Federal or state eligibility criteria, none of the government's seventy-two antipoverty programs is directed specifically toward meeting the needs of the poor.

In still other programs, the fact that benefits may overlap doesn't count. Nobody asks. For example, the value of free school breakfasts and lunches is not taken into account in figuring out how many food stamps a family can get. Is it heartless to suggest that the same child shouldn't be fed the same meal twice? Not at all. The object is to get the most benefits to the poorest people at the least cost to the taxpayers. It is not our objective to load up a lucky few with oversized benefits while others go hungry and the taxpayers go broke. The overlapping of programs and the duplication of benefits is inexcusable when you consider that a low-income family consisting of a mother and two children, one an infant and the other in school, is eligible simultaneously for 17 of the 44 major national welfare programs. Adding a father to the family raises the number of possible programs to 26. Then adding a teenaged child and a grandfather, the family becomes theoretically eligible for 35 of the 44 programs.

A welfare mother and her children could receive benefits simultaneously from the following 17 programs:

113

1. Child Nutrition
2. Food Stamps
3. Special Supplemental Food
4. Special Milk
5. Lower Income Housing Assistance
6. Rent Supplements
7. Public Health Services
8. Medicaid
9. Public Assistance Grants
10. Work Incentive
11. Employment Service
12. Financial Assistance for Elementary and Secondary Education
13. Public Assistance Services
14. Human Development Services
15. ACTION Domestic
16. Legal Services
17. Community Services

Overlap is almost universal among the 44 major welfare programs, since only 5 of them restrict eligibility on the basis of participation in other programs. Even where overlapping eligibility is considered, the recipient is not usually excluded from participating in all other programs, but rather is excluded from only a few other programs. In fact, many programs, and especially the basic cash-assistance programs—Aid for Families with Dependent Children (AFDC), Supplemental Security Income (SSI), Social Security, and Unemployment Compensation—encourage applicants to compound their benefits by applying for overlapping programs.

There is also the fact that the government's ancient computers and slipshod practices create a high error rate. For instance, in 1983 there was a 3 percent error rate for Medicaid, 4 percent for AFDC, and nearly 9 percent for food stamps.

Outrageous as it may seem, some 42.4 percent of those

receiving poverty benefits in 1981 had total incomes which were above 150 percent of the poverty level. In 1981, 150 percent of the poverty level for a family of four equaled $13,930 a year, which is just below what the Labor Department considered the average income of a typical lower-middle-income urban family that year. It is simply scandalous that we should so badly misdirect our poverty aid. It means almost half of the beneficiaries of poverty programs aren't really poor.

Yet another reason for the lack of results from our antipoverty programs is the ineffective management of the whole effort. The sheer number of programs, decentralization of responsibilities, lack of coordination among administrative and legislative functions, all add up to a lack of control within the government. But you also have to add in the complex, inconsistent, and sometimes conflicting eligibility criteria of so many income transfer programs. Many of the Federal agencies providing antipoverty benefits are unable to determine the administrative costs associated with those benefit programs. No private company could operate for very long without knowing its overhead costs.

The goal of lifting the poorest out of poverty has given way to the idea of bringing people up to the low- or even middle-income levels. Why? For one thing, it's a good way to keep the poverty industry going at full steam for a long time. The limited goal of bringing everyone above the poverty line could be quickly achieved with the current level of Federal spending. The huge market for the poverty industry is made up of those people who are not yet earning "middle-income" wages. But can we afford this tremendous expansion of redistribution?

The government apparently knows little about incentives to get poor people to work. When they work, their benefits get reduced, and this represents a "negative incentive." For example, a Congressional report said a Pennsylvania mother with two children would have to make about $10,000 a year to get the same income after taxes and work expenses as she was already getting from welfare plus food stamps and Medicaid. The typical welfare mother may not be able to get a job making $10,000 a year, especially if she's been at home caring for her kids for a long stretch.

So we see innumerable ways of not giving taxpayers' money to the truly poor. Little wonder that the poverty rate doesn't diminish, despite our sixfold increase in real poverty spending since 1959. No wonder the TV networks can go out and find plenty of cases to prove that we need to spend a lot more to eliminate poverty. The solution is plain. We must start directing our poverty programs to the poor.

We should redefine our poverty statistics to include in-kind Federal aid such as food stamps and rent subsidies. This would more accurately show who the truly needy are, and allow us to establish priorities in our poverty programs. Once we close the poverty gap, then we can worry more about those who are just above the poverty line. Let's eliminate the real poverty first.

We recommended that a form similar to a W-2 form (the one you file with your taxes) be issued to every recipient of a government subsidy of any kind. All the Federal payments shown on the form would be added to the beneficiary's earnings to arrive at his or her total income. Doing so would provide a concrete indication of which targeted outlays are meeting their objectives.

Better government computer systems (chapter 8) could also help. If the Federal government agencies involved in anti-poverty programs had common computerized accounting systems, we could get a clear picture of who is getting what benefits, and who is missing out. The computers could match benefits with recipients across all the agencies—something not now possible. In addition, better accounting systems are needed so these agencies will at last get a handle on how much they're spending to administer these programs.

The government ought to consolidate many of its more than 400 transfer programs, to cut down the overhead costs of each, and to keep better track of where the money's going. The key to reducing real poverty is in closely targeting anti-poverty money, so that not just 30 cents of the antipoverty dollar gets to poor people, but 90 cents or more. Our inefficiency in cutting poverty, despite massive Federal spending, is inexcusable.

We calculate that improved targeting of the means-tested income transfer programs could save up to $58.9 billion over three years. Cutting the administrative costs of the agencies would save even more, but these potential savings haven't been included in our savings estimates. We also need to define just what we mean when we discuss welfare programs. For example, the single largest welfare program (Social Security) isn't even generally recognized as a "welfare program."

On the Backs of Our Children

Many of the great social programs were initiated during the Great Depression. Social Security was created to help the elderly in their retirement years, along with whatever savings and other private pensions they may have received. Whatever the original intent, Social Security now pays benefits to eligible participants whether they need it or not.

The popular perception, or rather misconception, is that Social Security is self-supporting, with payments to beneficiaries met through payments to trust funds set up to meet the financial obligations of Social Security programs.

Social Security is not a pay-as-you-go program; that 7 percent that comes out of your paycheck every week does not come close to covering the ever increasing payments made. In 1983 alone, program payments of $168 billion exceeded Trust Fund receipts of $148 billion by $20 billion. This is an annual occurrence.

117

All current contributors to Social Security are, in effect, subsidizing all current recipients, since the benefits paid out are far in excess of the amounts paid in, including employee and employer contributions. Social Security beneficiaries who retired in 1981 receive more than 75 percent of their benefits in the form of a subsidy. Over a lifetime, the benefits received will be over four times the total contribution made by the employee and employer, plus interest on these contributions. Of the total Social Security payments of $168 billion in 1983, three-quarters, or $128 billion, represent subsidies to recipients.

As was true of the means-tested programs, Social Security payments (which are three-quarters subsidy) do not go exclusively to those in need. In this case, let's define the "poverty gap" as the amount by which the incomes of elderly Americans are below the government's official poverty level. In 1982, it would have cost $44 billion to raise the elderly poor as a group to the official poverty level. But after total social insurance program payments (including Medicare and Railroad Retirement) to the elderly of $160 billion were made, the poverty gap was still $3 billion. Over $119 billion in payments to the elderly did not affect the elderly poor. Who gets the money? Many of these payments go to those who may be marginally above official poverty definitions. However, a good deal goes to middle- and upper-class recipients, those for whom the threat of poverty in old age is more remote. It bears repeating: Approximately three-quarters of all social insurance payments to the elderly—mainly Social Security—are made to those above the poverty level. Since over three-quarters of the benefits paid are over and above contributions, they can be viewed as subsidies to elderly Americans, many of whose incomes exceed the poverty level.

These social insurance programs for the elderly will place an unconscionable burden on future generations and have gone beyond their original intent of providing a basic stan-

dard of living for the elderly. The system is a mess, and getting worse.

The President's Private Sector Survey recommendations
regarding Social Security were intended to improve the operational efficiency of Social Security Administration (SSA)
programs; we didn't look at the system with a view to change
policy. Legitimate payments, as required by current law,
would not be reduced one nickel as a result of these recommendations.

For example, erroneous payments of $14.6 billion were
made between 1980 and 1982. You've heard some of the stories about payments to dead people, and so on. However, even
when identified and repaid, these errors are costly. Assuming
a 10 percent interest rate, the estimated overpayments of
$14.6 billion cost the government $1.46 billion in interest.

The Social Security Administration already has the power
to sharply reduce erroneous payments. To determine the
amount for which a beneficiary is eligible, an Annual Earnings Test, showing the applicant's alternative sources of income, must be submitted. In general, overpayments do not
result from inaccurate reporting of income, but because some
beneficiaries fail to report income at all.

SSA should computerize data on all Old Age and Survivors Insurance (OASI) beneficiaries aged 62 to 69, as well as
on all Disability Insurance (DI) recipients, to monitor current
earnings. This would allow more timely identification of overpayments to OASI beneficiaries and would also bring to light
any Disability Insurance recipients who are working and are
therefore, by definition, not eligible for DI payments.

SSA should also require prospective income estimates
from beneficiaries so that benefits could be adjusted in a
timely manner, thus reducing overpayments. To encourage
accurate income estimating, SSA should exercise its existing
authority to charge interest on overpayments. SSA could reduce costs by $3 billion and increase revenues by another

billion dollars over three years, a combined total of $4 billion—if PPSS recommendations were adopted.

There are 4,852 SSA field offices, 70 percent of which are contact stations manned by staffs of three to six employees, who are expected to be well versed in all SSA programs. However, as the number and complexity of SSA-administered programs has grown, this has become less and less possible. We found that the personal contacts made at these stations could be handled just as easily over the phone, and 4,352, or 90 percent, of SSA field offices and contact stations could be consolidated into larger district offices. This would reduce personnel and overhead costs by $287 million over three years, an amount equivalent to the Social Security taxes paid by 177,709 median-income families in 1983.

You might ask, as we did, why consolidation hasn't been effected in the past. PPSS found that many SSA managers have submitted consolidation plans which have been rejected due to political considerations. Closing 4,352 offices in Congressional districts across the nation has political ramifications that tend to overwhelm the financial benefits no matter how obvious they may be.

While the PPSS review concentrated on major areas of potential savings, smaller, more specific possibilities in the Social Security Administration were also examined. For example, we found that SSA's Program Operations System includes a 25,000-page manual that is maintained by approximately 45,000 employees—SSA supervisors, claims analysts, and so on. It is intended to cover all contingencies related to the processing of an SSA claim. To put the amount of paper involved in perspective, if all 45,000 recipients of this manual stacked their copies atop one another, the pile would be 34 miles high. There are 12,000 pages of revisions to this manual each year, which means 12,000 pages for each of 45,000 manuals, or 540 million pages per year that need to be replaced. (On average, each employee has to insert new pages at a rate

120

of 60 pages per day.) Largely as a result of this manual, SSA printing and reproduction costs have increased at a rate of 12.5 percent per year from 1972 to 1982 to $21 million.

It was readily apparent that all 45,000 recipients of this manual do not need the level of detail provided. PPSS recommended that a less detailed version of this manual, of about 1,000 pages, be distributed to most employees to handle day-to-day problems, while an unabridged version be distributed to about 2,000 supervisory employees. Savings of $83 million over three years could be obtained.

The Bottom Line

In large measure, then, the problem of big government is the problem of big Transfer Programs—programs grown vastly larger in size and scope than ever envisioned when they were first put on the books. Using the government's terminology, "Payments for Individuals" were a record $402.5 billion in 1983, accounting for more than half of the entire Federal budget. By contrast, spending on national defense, considered the most important Federal function, was at $194.6 billion, less than half the "Payments for Individuals."

The whole subject of "Payments for Individuals" is so important that it has to be viewed in the context of past, present, and projected spending—their growth since 1962, before the proliferation of Great Society programs, to the present, and then out to the year 2000, only sixteen years away.

"Payments for Individuals" in 1962 were $29.6 billion, with Social Security and Veterans Benefits accounting for $19.6 billion or 66.2 percent of the total. Adding net interest, which is largely the result of the deficits we incur to finance these programs, we get a total of $36.5 billion in 1962, equal to 6.7 percent of GNP and 80.0 percent of the personal income taxes paid that year.

By 1983, "Payments for Individuals" rose to $402.5 billion,

121

13.6 times their 1962 amounts and, with net interest, took 15.3 percent of our GNP, 2.3 times their 1962 share. "Payments for Individuals" and the government's interest expense cost us 70.3 percent more than all the personal income taxes paid. And this came about despite the massive boost to these taxes from bracket creep—inflation pushing us into higher tax brackets.

Moreover, Social Security and Veterans Benefits, which accounted for nearly two-thirds of all "Payments for Individuals" in 1962, accounted for less than half—48.6 percent—in 1983, with the remaining 51.4 percent composed mainly of welfare programs that were quite small or nonexistent in 1962.

For example, Medicare, which did not even exist in 1962, was second only to Social Security at $56.9 billion in 1983. Supplemental Security Income, which also did not exist in 1962, cost us $8.7 billion in 1983. Taken together, these two programs accounted for $65.6 billion or 16.3 percent of "Payments for Individuals" in 1983. We thus have two programs— which did not even exist in 1962—having combined 1983 outlays of $65.6 billion, 2.2 times all "Payments for Individuals" in 1962.

Similarly, Food Stamps, which was a pilot program spending a mere $10 million in 1962, exploded to $11.8 billion in 1983, 1,180.0 times its 1962 level.

The outlook for the year 2000 is for "Payments for Individuals" to increase to $2.4 trillion, 6.1 times the 1983 level. The aging of the U.S. population as the baby boomers mature ensures that outlays for medical care and Social Security will rise faster than the overall economy between now and the year 2000. Indeed, Data Resources, Inc. (DRI) projects that almost one-quarter—24.7 percent—of GNP in the year 2000 will go to meet "Payments for Individuals" and the governments interest expense, or about the same percent of GNP that *total* Federal outlays take currently.

DRI also estimates that net interest on the debt will be $1.5 trillion in the year 2000, 16.9 times its present level. "Payments for Individuals" and interest expense are expected to reach $3.96 trillion in 2000, 2.5 times the $1.61 trillion in personal income taxes projected for that year.

The reality facing us in the year 2000 will be even worse than these projections if, as occurred during 1962–1983, programs not now in existence explode to require massive Federal spending by the year 2000.

What does it mean? The end of freedom as we, our parents, and our grandparents have known it—freedom we've fought wars to protect, we're now throwing away because we tolerate the insidious erosion of our liberties by the uncontrolled growth in government: growth fueled by the empty promises of politicians, the consequences of which we will have to explain to our children. Remember, economic freedom and political freedom are irrevocably linked—you can't have one without the other.

Chapter 8

It's a Long Way to Silicon Valley

The Tortoise and the Hare

Everyone has heard by now that we are living in the Information Age. Society has become Information-Intensive. Our nation is being transformed from an industrial economy to a service economy based on our ability to manipulate massive amounts of information. The wealth of cities such as New York, Los Angeles, and Chicago now rests on their high-level information industries.

Over three-quarters of the Federal white-collar work force is involved in the processing of information—from mailing Social Security payments to processing tax returns, vast amounts of data must be efficiently and effectively handled. A law passed by Congress, for example, directs the government to pay military retirees a certain amount of money each month based on their active-duty earnings and years of service. The function of the Executive Branch, then, is to figure out who these retirees are, how much they are to receive, and when and where to send the checks. Finally, it must draw the checks and get them into the hands of those retirees. This is almost entirely information processing. From the massive transactions-processing work done in agencies like the Internal Revenue Service and the Social Security Administration to the Pentagon's military command systems, the government depends on computers. Today, there is absolutely no operation of the Federal government—administrative, scientific, or military—that does not require the effective and efficient functioning of computer hardware and software.

The Federal government is the single largest user of data processing systems in the world. It operates over 17,000 computers, maintained by more than a quarter of a million government workers. More than 6,000 of the government computers are big general-purpose mainframes used for administrative functions, such as check processing. The other 11,000 computers are linked into special-purpose systems, similar to those used to control our nuclear defenses. More than 5 million separate programs are run on these computers.

These are approximate figures, because many government departments simply don't know how many computers they have. For instance, not only doesn't the Army know how many computers it has, it doesn't know where they are, how much has been spent on them, and whether or not they should be maintained, upgraded, or replaced (the estimate is that the Army spends between $2.5 and $3 billion a year on its systems). In any case, the Federal government's overall computer-related costs are about $12 billion a year, but that's just an estimate, too. The cost of maintaining these systems is unknown, because the government's accounting systems do not provide that information.

Since the Federal government is so deeply involved in data processing, you'd think it would be on the very leading edge of computer technology. You'd think it would run only the best, most sophisticated equipment. You'd think that several government agencies would be closely in touch with the latest developments in Silicon Valley, perhaps as active participants in the more advanced projects of the American computer industry.

If you thought any of these things, you'd be wrong. Federal government computers are an average of 6.7 years old. That doesn't sound old, but in the world of high-tech, it's ancient.

In private business, the average age of computers is about three years. As we have pointed out, one half the government's computers are so old that their manufacturers no longer provide service for them. The ability of departments to update their systems in a timely manner varies greatly. For instance, the average age of computers at the State Department is four years, versus eight years in the Navy and nine years at the Department of Transportation.

Matters are complicated by the fact that the government's computers can't talk to each other. Most are incompatible. For instance, the New York regional office of the Department of Health and Human Services alone uses ten different brands of incompatible computers. Not surprisingly, the welfare bureaucrats can't cross-check welfare programs to see who's getting what benefits, and who shouldn't be getting what benefits. This kind of needless incompatibility offers an open invitation to abuse and to defraud government programs.

You might suppose that this backwardness could have resulted from a laudable cost-conscious mentality on the part of government managers. However, it isn't out of frugality that obsolete computers are maintained. Just the opposite. The government has to have a special work force of computer technicians just to service antiquated data processing equipment. That alone raises the cost of government computer personnel to 41 percent of computer-related spending, compared to the 36 percent found in the private sector. This difference represents an added cost of $1 billion over three years.

These old and often obsolete computers, many of them still in the punch-card age (do not bend, staple, or fold), waste millions of taxpayer dollars a year. Here are some ways they do it: The Army Corps of Engineers, for example, has twenty-year-old computers that were obsolete before they were even installed in the early 1960s. They are extremely inefficient. In fiscal 1980, the Corps spent a million dollars to maintain these relics but got little for their money. For example, one district spent $127,000 over twenty months to keep its computer running, and used it at a rate of only two hours per month. At that rate of use, the Corps was spending $3,175 per hour to use the system.

Antique computers at the Census Bureau are a major part of the reason it took that office nearly four years to process data from the 1980 census, at a cost of $1.1 billion. The lateness of the census makes its information much less useful than it could be; by the time it's published, it may be outdated. Lacking sophisticated computer systems, the Census Bureau must check, edit, and account for the 88 million census questionnaires that were processed for the 1980 census— *by hand*. That alone required 37,000 clerks and cost more than $48 million. Since that part of the work came in 45 percent over budget at the Census Bureau, the agency then relaxed its editing standards to reduce the work load.

That relaxation could only have an adverse effect on the quality of the data. This matters, because census data are crucial to economists, demographers, scholars, and researchers of all sorts as they track trends in our population. Social and economic forecasters would be lost without these data. When you read in the newspaper that we are becoming a nation of single people, or that the birthrate has turned up, you're reading an analysis of census data.

The government wasn't always so backward. During the early 1960s, the U.S. Government was actually the leader in state-of-the-art computer hardware and software. But through the late 1960s and 1970s, the government fell far behind, because it failed to acquire common, centralized computer systems, and because the very procedure for buying systems is complicated and slow.

This is a most important obstacle to the efficient functioning of the government, and something for taxpayers to take note of. In the private sector, even in millions of private American homes, the computer revolution is rapidly transforming life, making all sorts of work easier and therefore more profitable. Those of you with your own personal computers are probably aware of this. Even if you don't have one yet, you will have noticed the hundreds of new computer publications in the bookstores and at the newsstands. You will have seen the ads and feature articles in the daily newspapers.

Look at what private industry has done with computers: The Atlantic Richfield Company installed a mainframe computer system in one of its departments, with personal computers spread through the offices, all tied into the mainframe. This system cost $271,186 and allowed employees to do word processing, electronic filing, printing, mailing, message sending, and preparation of graphs from their desks. Atlantic Richfield found that the new system saved the company $185,000 a year. Westinghouse looked into how new computers could improve white-collar productivity and tested computer records management, teleconferencing, word processing communications, telephone dictation, facsimile transmission, electronic mail, and other such technologies. Westinghouse found savings of over $150 million, plus better customer service and improved working conditions for its employees.

Or look at Owens-Illinois: Its Composite Can Products Group put in an IBM system to send invoice data over telephone lines from eight plants all over the country to headquarters in Toledo. That cut down to nothing the seven- to ten-day wait required when bills had to be sent by mail. As a result, the computer system paid for itself within a year. IBM itself saved $360,000 in the first six months when its General Systems Division started using electronic mail via computer. A word processing system saved Boeing Military Airplane Company $483,000 in the first nine months of use. The U.S. Insurance Group, a division of Crum & Foster, installed 147 word processing terminals, and the time saved was worth between $12,000 and $16,000 per operator.

One reason advanced by Federal officials for not upgrading government computers is possible "trauma" to current users of existing ADP systems. Most of us don't like change. We're not comfortable with it. But we adapt. We learn to substitute the word processor for the typewriter, the calculator for the adding machine. Change is all around us and we live with it. The government, however, in regard to its computer systems, has concluded that the economic and psychological costs of upgrading are simply not worth it.

If you work for the Federal government, you may respond that your office does have word processing computers (many don't) and perhaps even electronic mail systems (few do). True, but our Survey found that, in almost every case, the government's office automation systems are badly mismanaged. By its own estimate, government can save $12 billion annually through productivity gains from using microcomputers. But the same managers and programmers charged with upgrading the obsolete mainframes and twenty-year-old software are instructing users of the new microcomputers. They adapt the newer, more efficient computers to handle the old, poorly written software. The same twenty-year-old programs are processed at a faster rate. No real gain is achieved. They are typically not managed as systems or networks but rather on a stand-alone basis. Instead of bringing employees and information together, the government's computer system further isolates their users. The purchase of these systems is subdivided down to the office level, so there's no coordination within an agency, and certainly none with other agencies that might find it useful to share information. Government agencies routinely buy incompatible or duplicative computing systems. This makes it impossible to get the most out of the equipment, so it is often unutilized or underutilized. In 1976, the Federal Aviation Administration paid $4 million for new data terminal equipment that has never been installed because it was purchased without a clear idea of what its operational requirements would be. The Transportation Department, in another example, contracted out $18 million in computer time-sharing services in 1982 even while the Department's own computers were being used at as little as 20 percent of their capacity.

Besides rudimentary word processing, the government also does some telecommunicating—sending computer-generated text files and electronic mail messages via computer over phone lines. But mostly Federal personnel operate primitive setups that are slow and use telephone time inefficiently. Doing it the "old-fashioned" way, via voice telephone lines and a modem as the home computerist does, is okay for occasional users who have no reason to set up a more efficient system, but the Federal government ought to be taking advantage of the most advanced methods, such as using high-speed multiple-user circuits and such.

Walking Down an Up Escalator

Why can't the Federal government take advantage of computer technology to gain a vast, wholesale improvement in efficiency while reducing costs? Private business computer experts agree that computer hardware more than five years old does not perform at maximum efficiency. And with new, improved models coming out literally every day, even the five-year life-span is perhaps too optimistic. As for software, which is the programming that allows computers to do so many interesting things, the best new software is designed for the newest hardware.

Of course, the government does have some plans to replace its computers. A plan was put forward to replace 1,024 computers over the next five years. But that plan will actually worsen the situation in regard to the age of its computers. Even assuming the ones replaced are the oldest and an equal number are replaced each year, by the end of the plan, the average age of the government's computers will not be 6.7 years but 10.1 years, which is unacceptable.

Why such a slow pace? Well, to put in a new computer system at a government agency, you don't just figure out what you need, shop around, and then buy a system. Instead, you have to spend up to four years untangling red tape. During that time you must: Identify Requirements, Complete Conversion Study, Complete Cost-Benefit Study, Obtain Office of Management and Budget Approval, Obtain General Services Administration Approval, Complete Request for Proposal, Complete Benchmark Package (using some standard to compare the relative worthiness of a new system), Advertise in the Commerce Business Daily, Release the Request for Proposal and Benchmark Package, Review Proposals, Conduct Benchmark Tests, Request Best and Final Bids, Complete Evaluations, Award Contract, Settle Protests, inform Congress and/or obtain Congressional approval, and, finally, Install New Equipment.

Now, once you've done all this, chances are the computer system you're buying is already years out of date. About 60 percent of the computers bought by the government first came on the market four years prior to the purchase, and a fifth of them came on the market eight years before they were bought. So roughly 80 percent of the government's computers are out of date before they are installed.

It used to be, in the 1960s, that the Federal government had some of the best computer people in the country. That is now past history. Here's one place, among many others, where the Federal government is penny-wise and pound-foolish. It may try to attract the best computer experts to run its systems, but it can't. Computer professionals are at a premium these days. Turnover is high, even in private industry, where about one-fifth of these workers change jobs every year, always moving up the ladder. Many of the best computer people in the government have left to go into private industry. They have been lured there by better salaries, and the considerable attraction of being able to work with much more sophisticated equipment, which is crucial to their career development.

Mediocre Federal computer pay makes it prohibitively difficult to hire good people. Data processing is one area where Federal pay lags behind the private sector. In data processing, it trails pay in the private sector at all levels, and by 25 percent in the upper levels. The Federal government offers entry-level computer personnel a salary of about $14,000 a year while they can get more than $20,000 to start in the private sector. Top-level computer executives are discouraged by the government's salary cap of approximately $60,000 a year—much less than they can make in private industry. To compound the problems of maintaining an effective ADP work force, the Office of Personnel Management is currently in the process of downgrading salary scales for computer personnel.

Some government officials argue that, yes, the pay is lower, but the retirement benefits are very attractive (as discussed in chapter 5). But highly qualified young professionals don't take a job because of the retirement benefits. They don't expect, nor should they expect, to stay in a lower-level job all their working lives. They are ambitious and expect to move up fast in an open-ended career. No surprise, then, when the Social Security Administration recently launched a recruiting effort to fill six hundred data processing positions and received only a handful of applications. Thus, the Social Security Administration's system modernization project, which is expected to save $8.5 billion over five years, is put in serious jeopardy.

Even if a computer technician accepts the lower pay, he is often put off by the drawn-out procedures for hiring. Before he or she can be considered for a government job, each candidate has to be "examined" and then "certified." It can take more than a year. It's a frustrating process for the government manager who's doing his best to get qualified people. Good candidates take other jobs in private business while the Federal manager is unable to make a job offer. The government simply offers too little, too late, and so is out of the running.

The Blind Man and the Elephant

Beyond computer hardware, the software is critical. Software is the programming that tells computers exactly what to do, literally by the numbers. Suffice to say that the Federal government operates 332 different accounting systems and over 100 payroll systems. Each agency has developed its own accounting software. This means that government managers confront a growing information gap caused by incompatible records, leaving them without the kind of information they need to operate efficiently.

For instance, because data sources aren't coordinated and centrally available, government loan managers don't have the information to monitor repayments and follow up on loan delinquencies. Better information would be the first step in reducing the $35 billion in receivables that were overdue at the end of 1982. The Education Department doesn't have the figures it needs to keep tabs on the $7 to $8 billion it makes available each year in student loans. Government social programs can't effectively verify the incomes of poverty aid recipients, with the result that annual overpayments of over $4 billion are made. Lack of common accounting software assures that the scope, cost, and impact of the government's various food programs are simply unknown. The Veterans Administration pays out $15 billion a year in benefits, and it is estimated that its error rate is in excess of half a billion dollars a year.

133

A Success Story or Two

A handful of government agencies are exceptions to the rule. The State Department has the newest computers in the Federal government. Its computers are only 3.8 years old—still older than most private-industry computers, but positively brand-new by Federal standards. Furthermore, the State Department's computers are standardized. They are laid out in a network, so that individual State Department people can work on personal computers that are tied into one central mainframe. That's the way it is supposed to be.

The FBI is another part of the government that seems to be on the right track in information technology. Though its computers are roughly six years old, the FBI has managed to cut the purchasing lag to four months in some cases. When the FBI recently decided to buy a new computer, it began the acquisition process in February and actually installed the computer by June of the same year. That's good even by private sector standards. It's unheard-of in the Federal government, where the average computer acquisition cycle takes two and a half to four years.

What led to this success at the State Department and the FBI? For one thing, both agencies use an ongoing, long-range planning process closely tied to yearly budgeting. Both agencies have realized that they need good, highly trained computer professionals, and they have taken steps to attract qualified personnel. Both closely check on the efficiency of their computer systems. And both agencies use professionals to oversee the purchase, installation, and operation of their computers.

Catching Up on the Revolution

We are truly in the midst of a revolution, and, in the last two decades, computer technology has had a profound

134

impact on American management. In the next decades, it will have a greater impact, in ways we cannot now foresee. The technology of the information age is open-ended, making it more powerful than past revolutionary technologies such as that of the internal combustion engine. Of course, change is always frightening. It brings with it uncertainty as to who will profit, and who will lose.

Our survey showed that at least $22.6 billion could be saved over three years, after accounting for implementation costs, and that just scratches the surface. The government needs to replace its obsolete models, and get new ones that tie in with each other, so the different agencies can share information. There is a dire need for payroll, accounting, and management information software that is compatible throughout the agencies of government.

The government sorely needs to start offering computer professionals competitive pay. It should also make upgraded computer systems, especially microcomputers, available not only to secretaries and typists but to managers and high-level analysts. The General Services Administration should give the agencies greater leeway in buying and leasing computers.

Finally, we recommend that the government set up an Information Management Office inside the Executive Office of the President. To run the office, it should hire a top, executive-level computer professional and put him in charge of all the government's computer operations to ensure government-wide coordination and policy direction. He in turn would oversee a newly hired corps of senior government data processing professionals, one at each agency.

If the Federal government reformed its information processing so that it had the right kind of data systematically entered on up-to-date, compatible computers, running common software applications, this would go a long way to reducing the Federal "information gap," which the survey estimated costs the government $78.6 billion over three years.

135

Chapter 9

Going Private

How Wild Is San Francisco?

In 1825, when Army posts were isolated fortresses out on the wild frontiers of America, the government found it necessary to let the Army set up small grocery stores inside the posts, to sell supplies at cost to its officers. This was a convenience, so they wouldn't have to be riding into town every day to buy sourdough, beef jerky, and Kentucky whiskey. By 1866, the Congress decided to let the enlisted men in on this commissary service. These government grocery stores were entirely separate from the famous PXs, the post exchanges where military families can buy everything from cigarettes to vacuum cleaners at discount.

Today, military commissaries number 358, of which 238 are in the continental U.S. They employ nearly 25,000 people and do $4.2 billion of business a year. Such an isolated outpost as Washington, D.C., has six of them. Wild frontier towns like San Francisco and San Antonio have five. Remote San Diego and forlorn Norfolk, Virginia, have four. Honolulu, a cruel hardship post, has three, and so on. At least 109 of the military commissaries are located in urban areas of the U.S. The Army alone operates 141 of them, with a staff of 10,935. In the U.S., taxpayers subsidize the commissary system with over three-quarters of a billion dollars a year. This is because the 5 percent surcharge added to each item sold does not cover all operating expenses, and because some operating costs are "hidden" under other appropriations.

The chairman of the House Armed Services Committee, about 1949, declared after an extensive investigation that the whole theory and sole justification of the commissaries was to serve only those military personnel who were stationed at isolated posts, miles from any other grocery stores. Thus, he concluded, what made sense in the days of stagecoaches and Indian ambushes no longer makes sense today, when grocery stores abound, and isolation is mostly a state of mind—it was never intended that commissaries replace private grocery stores.

Even Congress has from time to time recognized this obvious fact. Since 1953 it has required each commissary to justify its continuing existence every three years by a certification process. In theory, this ought to guarantee that every commissary that still exists deserves to. But Congressional theory rarely works out in real life, and this is no exception.

Certification requires that each commissary show that the local military base is at least fifteen minutes away from any commercial grocery store, or that the commercial food stores lack the necessary variety and selection of products, or that the local grocery store prices are at least 20 percent higher than prices at the commissary. But in reality, commissary managers can easily manipulate the certification process. For example, commissary managers know in advance what items will be compared in price to those in the private grocery stores, so they can negotiate special deals to make sure those prices are lower. Further, they can select the two stores to which their prices are compared, and can even select the day of the survey, thus avoiding private-sector sale days when the best prices are offered.

137

In any case, the price comparison excludes the inexpensive generic and house brand items sold in many private grocery stores, and compares only a limited group of expensive brand-name items. Cigarettes, which are sold tax-free in the commissaries, are given extraordinarily heavy weight in the surveys—in one survey, cigarettes represented 7.1 percent of the items surveyed, although they are only 4.1 percent of sales in the average supermarket. A major part of the "savings" revealed in the surveys comes merely from the fact that cigarettes are exempt from Federal excise taxes in commissaries. For instance, a 1980 study at one Air Force base showed cigarette savings of 37 percent, of which 15 percent resulted from the lack of taxes. Store managers can also play with the fifteen-minute requirement, since it is based on driving time rather than distance. And in fact, a General Accounting Office study found that approximately 84 percent of the commissaries are within ten miles of at least two private supermarkets. There are all sorts of maneuvers by which the results of the certification process can be altered in favor of the commissaries.

Little wonder that not a single military commissary has ever been denied certification. The whole process amounts to a charade meant to placate any critics of the commissaries. All a Congressman has to do to "prove" that the commissaries in his district are justified is to refer to the latest certification results.

Not only are the military commissaries no longer justified as government entities, they are also grossly inefficient, competing with commercial grocery store chains, but without the profit motive. We found that in addition to $402.2 million a year in appropriated funds, the commissaries in the continental U.S. also cost $170.5 million in hidden expenses for things like maintenance of personnel files, garbage collection, computer time, and other overhead costs. Then add on the yearly $26.4 million in inventory carrying costs. To top it off, add in $114.7 million per annum in lost tobacco excise taxes, plus $43.9 million a year in lost sales taxes. Total loss to tax-payers from continental U.S. commissaries: $758 million per year.

The commissaries, despite all their subsidies, hidden costs, and exemptions from taxes, despite all this, offer savings no different from what you will find at most warehouse grocery stores—one of those newer kinds of low-overhead supermarkets offering top-quality brands. Both the commissaries and the warehouse supermarkets provide actual savings of about 20 percent below prices in traditional super-markets that offer Muzak, recessed lighting, bag boys, and other costly amenities. While warehouse grocery stores offer savings equal to those in commissaries, they receive no subsidy and still make a profit.

The defenders of the military commissaries, who are legion in Congress and at the Pentagon, insist that the commissary benefit is a major inducement for people to join the armed services. Not correct. Studies show that good pay is what attracts people to the services and keeps them there. The Congressional argument is absurd if you think about it. The argument assumes that the commissary privilege is a compensation for less money. First, military pay is at least equivalent to private-sector pay for similar positions. Second, why should anyone choose the option of receiving military pay along with a 20 percent food discount, when instead he could have civilian pay, and still get the food discount by shopping at a commercial warehouse supermarket?

The commissary stores, which exist on taxpayer subsidies and investment, constitute a separate, Federally run, retail food chain, immune to the laws of market supply and demand, free of the normal pressures to operate efficiently. They ought to be turned over to the private sector; that is, we ought to allow private companies to operate the commissaries. This would save many millions of taxpayer dollars, and free the

Pentagon from the diverting and arduous task of managing four parallel systems of grocery store chains (one for each branch plus the Marines). It would release 25,000 employees to do work more directly related to national security. It would free Congress and the Administration of the time and money spent overseeing the system. We calculate that the three-year savings which would result from allowing the private sector to run commissaries could exceed $2.4 billion.

Doing It Privately

There is a grand principle here, an exciting one. It is referred to as "privatization." It means the turning over of a government enterprise to the private sector, whether by selling it off lock, stock, and barrel, or contracting with the private sector to perform the service rather than doing it in-house. The word is well known in Europe, where the disastrous failure of nationalized companies has inspired some governments, notably that of Prime Minister Margaret Thatcher, to return them to private industry. Indeed, "privatization" has become a household word in Britain. British Airways, the state-owned airline, and British Telecom, the government telecommunications monopoly, are going private. Steel mills, auto plants, coal mines, and such have been turned over to private hands.

In the same way that military commissaries could be turned over to the private sector and could be run more effectively, there are many other government-produced goods and services that ought to be turned over or contracted out to private industry. This type of situation, in which the government has insulated itself from pressures to reduce waste and inefficiency, is repeated thousands of times throughout government. As a result, inefficiency abounds. Using the private sector to provide a government service introduces market efficiencies.

140

The Federal government performs an estimated 11,000 commercial activities, costing $20 billion a year and employing a quarter of the 1.9 million civilian Federal workers in the U.S. But just because government provides a good or service, there's no reason why it should also produce that good or service, especially when the private sector can provide better service at a lower cost. There are many reasons why government does not need to produce all the services it provides:

The paramount reason is that government-run enterprises lack the driving forces of marketplace competition, which promote tight, efficient operations. This bears repetition, because it is such a profound and important truth. In private business, you sink or swim in accord with whether your enterprise can operate efficiently enough so that its revenues exceed its costs, generating a profit that can reward those who risked their hard-earned money to back the enterprise. The only possible exception is the case of monopoly, which, like government, doesn't need to operate efficiently because it has the power to raise prices to cover inefficiency.

But if you search for monopolies with a sophisticated eye, you'll find that the only monopolies that endure are those that are monopolies by virtue of some government policy. For example, your local electric utility is probably a state-commissioned monopoly, overseen by a state regulatory board. Some uninformed critics of business would claim that a large corporation such as IBM is a "monopoly." Nonsense. IBM and every other large corporation face competition, in the U.S. and from overseas, and even from other kinds of products.

Besides their lack of competitiveness, government operations lack the kind of sophisticated information systems that would permit them to arrive at sound and efficient decisions. They've never developed good management information systems, probably because they've never been forced to by the pressures of competition. They're also tied up by strict regulations that don't allow them to manage effectively, such as

141

Civil Service rules that hinder hiring, firing, and pay decisions. This is disastrous to efficiency.

Also, the government operations that should be privatized are too often driven by political considerations more than economic ones. The question the government asks about its enterprises is not how efficient they are, but who benefits and—most important—how many voters support them. Their employees are judged not on how well they do their jobs, but on their seniority. They are directly controlled or strongly influenced by Congress, which ensures that effective management will be subordinated to political expediency. For example, can you imagine the chief of a $26-billion operation with over 200,000 employees having to get the approval of his board of directors for any reorganization plan that will affect as few as three employees—and who will have to wait eight months to enact that plan? No? Well, meet the Administrator of the Veterans Administration. That's what the law now requires him to do. Before it was passed, one Congressman explained that "This will allow Congress to monitor the VA offices and hospitals, which are of major concern to our veterans." Maybe, but that's no way to run an operation efficiently. In fact, we believe the VA hospital system is a fine candidate for privatization—reducing costs and improving services to our veterans.

We found that whenever you compare a service provided by the government to an identical one provided by the private sector, the private sector does it better. The main reason is that if you have an inefficient private-sector company, a better-managed, more efficient one comes along and grabs its market. That doesn't happen with a government enterprise. Federal managers have the ultimate safety net; they cannot fail financially. They are backed up in their inefficiency by powerful constituencies that lobby to prevent changes that may adversely affect their special interests. Then too, Federal managers are rewarded for inefficiency with higher budget appropriations and more staff. For example:

- Budget allocations are made to individual Veterans Administration hospitals on the basis of the number of patient-days each hospital records during the year, which creates an incentive to increase admissions and delay discharges until there is another patient to fill the vacated bed. Any hospital that fails to meet its target patient-day work load loses a portion of its budget appropriations.
- The stated purpose of military commissaries is to procure and resell food at the lowest possible cost. However, the managers' operating funds come from surcharge revenues, determined as a percentage of cost. Thus, managers can increase operating funds by paying higher prices for food procurement.

Even if they are inclined to improve efficiency, Federal managers don't usually possess the authority to be real managers. They have little authority to hire or fire or reward good performance. They don't have the management information systems that would enable them to make the best decisions. They have no license to make investments that would improve the enterprise over the long haul. What they end up doing is management by rote—going by the book, not making waves, following the letter of each regulation.

The Office of Management and Budget does have a mechanism for deciding whether a government service ought to be done in-house or contracted out. But it doesn't work too well. Rather than compare contractors' bids to established in-house costs for providing products or services, the OMB procedure is to compare in-house costs to theoretical costs. These theoretical costs are supposed to represent what hypothetical, ideal, most efficient in-house costs would be. Even if these ivory-tower "ideal" costs come out higher than what private contractors bid, still the rules say the difference must be at least 10 percent. So the deck is stacked against decisions to contract out services.

To develop these "ideal" costs, agencies do an extensive management review. You might think an agency would use the occasion to review its level of efficiency. Wrong. Inefficiency, incredibly, doesn't count in the management review. Federal managers are not reprimanded if the review uncovers and documents waste. The opportunity to shape up an agency by comparing its costs to those of outside contractors is lost.

Privatization also recognizes that the government possesses limited resources and must put them where it gets the maximum return on the dollar. Spending billions per year and tying up many thousands of government employees in operations that duplicate the private sector (but without the profit motive) is simply wasteful.

This isn't to say that government involvement in producing goods and services is always bad. There have been times when government has acted as a valuable catalyst in industry—when it had the sense to get out of a market once the market began to develop on its own (this is what the Japanese routinely do). When aviation was in its infancy, airplanes were novelties, too crude and unreliable for any sort of commercial service. No one knew if a market for commercial airplanes existed. To manufacture them, companies would have had to invest huge sums in sophisticated new technology before airplanes would be safe enough to fly on a regular basis.

The U.S. Government stepped in, gathering a huge array of talent to develop the airplanes needed to fight the First and Second World Wars. The most notable result was the C-47 cargo workhorse, which after the Second World War was known in civilian dress as the Douglas DC-3, the first viable commercial airliner, and one of the best-built planes ever to fly. Indeed, a few of them, reconditioned from the Second World War, are still flying.

After the war, a healthy new aviation industry was growing up, and government wisely got out of the business, putting its aviation resources into aerospace, at a time when space was in its infancy. And now that space shuttle flights have become routine, with the space industry on the edge of major growth, it is time for the government to let private business gradually take over there, too.

Local governments are way ahead of the Federal government in privatization, with outstanding results. For instance, the city of Scottsdale, Arizona, contracts out its fire protection to a private fire-fighting outfit, at an annual saving of $2 million. A private computer services firm runs the computers for Orange County, California, at an annual saving of $1.6 million to the taxpayers. Butte, Montana, saves some $600,000 per year by contracting out the running of its municipal hospital. Newton, Massachusetts, saves $500,000 by contracting out paramedical and ambulance services. Oakland, California, sold its museum and city auditorium to private investors for $55 million, in a leaseback arrangement whereby the investors are responsible for maintaining the property. Many cities use the private sector for garbage collection, tree-trimming, car-towing and the like. A 1982 survey found that of 1,780 cities and counties, 41 percent contracted out commercial waste collection, 34 percent residential waste, 30 percent tree care, 78 percent vehicle towing and storage, and 28 percent motor vehicle fleet management. As Pennsylvania Governor Dick Thornburgh put it: "If the states are truly 'laboratories of democracy' . . . then 'experiments' in these areas which have served them so well over the years should be transported to the Federal level without delay."

You may object that big business is advocating that the Federal government turn itself over to the private sector. In other words, it is a ploy for big business to get its hands on government operations so it can make more money while weakening the government. Privatization would have little effect on most large corporations. But it can be an opportunity for smaller companies and independent entrepreneurs to get in there and produce goods and services cheaper and better than the government. That is the way it has turned out at the local level. Actually, privatization of redundant and inefficient government services would be one good, unobtrusive way for the Federal government to stimulate the economy and give entrepreneurs new opportunities to start businesses. And when taxpayers save money in the process, there are no valid reasons to procrastinate bringing private-sector management, expertise, efficiency, and so forth, into government.

Privatization is not only good business sense, in some cases it is the only alternative to continuing inefficient government operations. With over 17,000 computers and a work force of more than 250,000, Federal computer operations dwarf those of even the largest private-sector users. During the early 1960s, the Federal government was the acknowledged leader in using state-of-the-art computer hardware and software. Yet, in the 1980s, approximately 50 percent of the government's ADP inventory is so old that it is no longer supported by the manufacturer and must be maintained by specially trained Federal personnel. The massive job of upgrading Federal ADP systems *requires* private-sector state-of-the-art involvement at many levels, from contracting for software and hardware to turning over entire operations to the private sector to operate. In privatizing ADP operations, the government does not abdicate responsibility, but allows a more efficient operation to produce the required information.

More Candidates for Privatization

Turning the military commissaries over to the private sector would be a good start, but there are plenty of other prime candidates. Indeed, we recommend that the Administration set up a full-time office to do nothing but scout for more possibilities for privatization, and put privatization into effect. For example:

Power to the Utilities. The Federal government is the world's largest producer of hydroelectric power. Its 123 hydroelectric plants, run by the Energy Department's Power Marketing Administration, supply nearly half of the nation's hydroelectric production, mostly in the West and South. But Federal budget outlays for this power production, including construction costs, have exceeded revenues in nearly every year since the program began in the 30s and 40s. The hydroelectric power production represents a long-term drain on the Federal budget, since the revenues aren't enough to pay back the government's large capital investment in hydroelectric power production. The accounting system devised by the Power Marketing Administration is so shoddy that no independent auditor will give the account books his stamp of approval.

The rates are very cheap for this government power. The government charges about 1.6 cents per kilowatt-hour wholesale, while private utilities charge an average of nearly 4 cents per kilowatt-hour—2.4 times as great. That's a great subsidy if you are served by one of the 956 Western or Southern state and local electric companies that buy Federal power. It isn't so great for the rest of us, who subsidize the low rates.

The Federal government got into this business a long time ago, when it built huge dams in poor parts of the country that didn't have investor-owned utilities to provide electricity. Now investor-owned utilities are everywhere, and there is simply no reason for the Federal government to be in the power-generating business. Since it is losing money in the business, there is plenty of reason for it to turn these operations over to the private sector.

147

Who would buy the power plants? State and local governments or electric co-ops. Why would they buy these assets? Because buying them would be far cheaper than building any type of new power production plant. In any case, they would be free to price the electricity thus generated so it covered costs. How much would this privatization save the taxpayer? A handsome $20 billion over a three-year span.

Big Profits in Outer Space. The outer space industry looks like the next major advanced technological frontier for business. It could be an important economic base for the U.S.—if we don't dissipate our leadership position, which we could well do unless we start encouraging private-sector participation in the space industry. Recently, Japanese and European semiprivate companies have started to move in on what has been an American market. For instance, Arianespace, a private company created and subsidized by the European Space Agency, has been undercutting NASA. They can do this because NASA requires payment in full before it will launch a company's communications satellite, but Arianespace only requires the bill to be paid when the satellite starts generating revenue. That's an awfully attractive deal. Such American companies as GTE and Western Union have signed up to have Arianespace launch their satellites.

The space business now consists of the burgeoning satellite industry, space-launching services, and "materials processing in space"; for example, the growing in space's weightless gravity of ultrapure silicon chips for use in computers, or the manufacture of lenses and certain drugs, done aboard a space station or shuttle flight. Right now, the greatest demand is for launches to put communications satellites in orbit, for use in television and telephone communications.

By the government's own estimate, its present space-launch capability (either through reusable space shuttles or expendable rockets) isn't sufficient to meet the demand for launches through the 1980s. Thus, very soon other nations will take up the slack, unless our private-sector companies are allowed to fill the unmet need.

The government ought to play a large role in space, but it can no longer do it all by itself. Federal budget amounts for civilian space activities keep getting smaller. The space budget is presently frozen at the already planned four space shuttles, though numerous studies insist that a fifth shuttle is strongly needed to meet space-launch demand. In addition, it's uncertain how long NASA will stay in the expendable rocket business.

Then too, private-sector investment in space will lessen the taxpayer burden. It will also quicken the pace of innovation, and likely introduce new efficiencies. The dynamism of the private market can perk the industry up. Space technology would very likely develop faster, because the private sector, spurred by profit-making competition, has the sort of management, marketing and finance flexibility that NASA can't attempt. NASA, after all, is part of the Federal government, dependent on the vagaries of the Federal budget as it wends its way through Congress.

How would space privatization work? Already, a private U.S. consortium called Space-Tran has proposed funding a commercial orbiter for up to $1 billion. It would like to buy a fifth space shuttle with private funds raised in the U.S., and contract it out on a commercial basis, with NASA providing flight-support services for a fee. Space-Tran would make the shuttle available for the Pentagon's use in an emergency.

The Fedex Space Transportation Co., a joint venture between Federal Express and the Martin Marietta Corp., manufacturer of the Titan rocket, has proposed sponsoring commercial satellite launches using expendable Titan III missiles.

These kinds of initiatives are vital if we are to stay ahead in space. Besides, we calculate that privatizing some space launches would trim the Federal budget by at least $1.5 billion over three years.

149

Private Hospitals for the VA. The Veterans Administration hospital system was started in 1921 because, back then, there weren't enough hospitals to care for the men wounded, maimed, and gassed in the First World War. The Second World War put even more strain on American hospitals, and Federal help was keenly needed. Today, the VA operates 172 hospitals, 93 nursing homes, 227 outpatient clinics, plus numerous other facilities. In fact, the VA operates the largest health care system in the United States.

But the VA facilities are nearing obsolescence despite some $3.1 billion spent on construction since 1974. Nearly three-quarters of the hospital beds are in hospitals built before 1955. Many are not air-conditioned, and they have large, open wards rather than semiprivate rooms. They lack safety features now considered standard in modern hospitals. Since it costs the VA approximately $258,400 for each new hospital bed, replacing the obsolete facilities would cost $33 billion over a twenty-year period.

Recently Duke University built a hospital similar to a VA one for $97,400 per bed, and the University of Florida built one for $122,800 per bed. The VA's cost on a comparable basis for a similar hospital facility was $208,000 per bed. It is the same story in nursing home construction: It costs the VA an average of $61,250 per bed, while Beverly Enterprises, a private nursing home chain, is able to build a nursing home bed for an average of $15,900—four times cheaper.

Why is VA construction so expensive? For one thing, padded overhead. The VA has a construction administration staff of eight hundred. Compare this with the fifty-person construction staff of the Hospital Corporation of America, a private company that runs three hundred hospitals and handles the same amount of hospital construction as the VA does each year. Besides making VA construction overhead four times as expensive as private-sector construction overhead, the bloated VA staff also slows construction down, so that it takes the VA seven years to finish a project, versus two years at HCA. Of course, time is money in the construction trade.

Another reason for the high cost of adding a new bed at the VA is simply the fact that the VA insists on using a rather rigid method of specifying how a hospital will be built; instead of specifying what the end result should be, thus giving building contractors flexibility in the use of materials, the VA imposes construction regulations that don't improve quality but do push up construction costs.

As for patient care in the VA hospitals, it costs approximately 18 percent more than in private hospitals. And, only 12 percent of veterans hospitalized in 1978 chose VA hospitals; 88 percent were admitted to non-VA hospitals.

Therefore, it would make a lot of sense to do the following: The VA should get out of the hospital construction business, contracting out the construction instead to private hospital construction firms, who do the job better and cheaper. For nursing homes, the VA should not build any homes not already under contract. Rather, it can turn underused hospital beds into nursing beds. If that doesn't suffice, the VA can contract more beds from private nursing homes. The VA also should try contracting out hospital management services in several of its hospitals. If that works, the VA could convert its whole hospital system to private management, at considerable savings and probably with better treatment of patients, too. We figure these measures would save $1.4 billion over three years.

Selling Off Washington's Airports. Washington, D.C., is a Federal district, and the Federal government owns both Washington National Airport, four miles from the White House, just across the Potomac in Virginia, and Dulles International Airport, twenty-five miles from Washington, way out in Loudon County, Virginia. Both are operated by the Federal Aviation Administration, which has better things to do, such as ensuring the flight safety of the nation's airways.

For fifty years, Congress and sundry Federal commissions have been proposing ways for the government to operate the airports more effectively and efficiently.

In 1981, these two airports had a cash operating deficit of $6.9 million. The deficit resulted largely from the below-market-price landing fees charged—Dulles charged no landing fees; National assessed landing fees of 43 cents per thousand pounds. This compares to landing fees of $2.34 per thousand pounds assessed at Newark Airport.

There's simply no reason for the Federal government to be in the airport business, and the airports would be better off run by local organizations that include aviation and community interests. Because the Washington airports have to depend on the yearly dice shoot of the Federal budget process for their funding, the airport management is discouraged from planning very far into the future. Thus Washington National and Dulles aren't easily able to finance improvements over the long term.

As it is now, the FAA finds itself both the regulator and the regulatee of airport procedure. You might think this could be beneficial, offering the FAA firsthand insight into the effects of its own regulations. Rather, it leads to confusion within the FAA. Thus the agency has in the past come out with proposals for transferring responsibility for the two airports to non-Federal entities.

According to our findings, Washington National and Dulles would be better off and the taxpayers would save $455 million over three years if we sold the airports to an independent local airports authority.

Getting the Lead Out. The Federal government runs a fleet of 436,000 cars, trucks, fire engines, buses, and other special vehicles. Some 80 percent are light trucks and sedans. The Defense Department operates the most vehicles, 138,000, and the Postal Service uses 118,000. These vehicles aren't run very efficiently. In fact, the government is unable to figure out exactly what the cars and trucks are costing per mile. The whole fleet is reported to cost well over a billion dollars a year to own and operate. However, the Federal statistical break-downs on actual fleet operations are so bad they are useless for management control.

We found that the government vehicles are mostly under-used, and this runs up their costs tremendously. For example, Hertz figures that it costs the company 45 cents a mile to operate a compact car 10,000 miles a year. But at 15,000 miles a year the cost drops to 34 cents per mile, and at 25,000 miles a year it falls to 26 cents a mile. The Federal fleet travels an average of less than 9,000 miles a year. So you'd expect fleet costs to be 45 cents a mile or more, especially since two-thirds of the fleet is made up of light trucks that are more expensive to run. The 1981 fleet report, however, shows the average fleet costs to be 36 cents per mile. Is the government suddenly so efficient? No. It just doesn't include all the costs in its analysis.

If Federal annual mileage used were raised from 9,000 to 15,000, over 200,000 vehicles could be dropped from the fleet. (Private-sector car-rental firms consider 25,000 miles to be effective annual usage.) Conservatively, we propose that the Federal fleet ought to be immediately reduced by 100,000 vehicles, to raise the utilization rate of the remaining ones, thus lowering their cost per mile. Next, the government ought to contract out both management of the fleet and garage re-pair, when cost-effective. Three-year savings would be $1.5 billion.

Rescuing the Coast Guard. We could save more than $1.2 billion over three years by contracting out some of the less essential tasks of the Coast Guard. The Coast Guard could save time and money by letting private tow boats handle non-life-threatening "search-and-rescue" operations, some 80 per-cent of which are within three miles of shore, and 72 percent of which involve recreational boats. The Coast Guard could also contract such chores as buoy maintenance and vessel inspection. This would free the Coast Guard to do more important work guarding our shorelines and waterways. The Coast Guard was never meant to be a babysitter and lifeguard for the nation's weekend sailors. This would also save $1.26 billion over three years.

Privatizing Small Stuff. The Social Security Administration runs three shifts, seven days a week, plus rented computer time, but still its ancient computers stay backed up for five and six weeks processing Social Security cards. There is also a three-year backlog in posting retirement contributions, and a backlog in processing 7.5 million new claims each year. This logjam could be solved by contracting out most of the computer work. That would also save a considerable amount of money. A 2 percent increase in productivity, for example, could save $100 million over five years.

The Pentagon set up the Uniformed Services University of the Health Sciences in 1972 to train medical students to become military doctors. But it costs $77,186 per year to train a student at the University, versus the $19,146 it costs through the Health Professions Scholarship Program, which in any case has been the main source of physicians for the military. There is no clear justification for the existence of the University. Closing it would save the taxpayers $117 million over three years.

The Postal Service issues 22.4 million checks annually, using a Treasury account that costs a bit over a dollar per check. If the Post Office used regular commercial bank accounts, it could get a rate as low as 10 cents a check. Even at 20 cents per check, the Postal Service could save $60 million over three years.

Let's Stop Giving Away the Store

There is another form of privatization that deserves

attention. We need to let private users share more of the burdens of government services, except in hardship cases. With
yearly budget deficits of $180–$200 billion to worry about,
the U.S. Government ought to price many of its free or "bar-
gain-basement priced" services to reflect the cost of the service. Instead, taxpayers unknowingly subsidize a wide range
of things from free firewood to free maps. Why shouldn't the
Forest Service collect modest entrance fees at the recreation
parks and camping sites that are now free? Why should all
taxpayers subsidize those relative few who choose to use our
national parks? In any case, when something like that is given
away free, you get into what economists call "the tragedy of
the commons," in which everyone uses a facility, say a camp-
ground, and since it is free no one feels any responsibility
toward its upkeep. "Someone else" will take care of that. So
often such Federal recreation facilities become broken-down,
litter-strewn eyesores.

It should be remembered that user charges, whether sufficient or insufficient, are paid by a discrete section of the population. For a broad range of government-provided commercial services, there is no justification for the population as a
whole—and for taxpayers as a group—to subsidize a small
section of clearly identifiable beneficiaries.

Here are some examples of how the government subsidizes sundry services, often for reasons that no longer make
sense:

The Army Corps of Engineers spends around $500 million
annually to dredge harbors for the benefit of commercial vessels. The Corps of Engineers likewise helps build and keep the
locks, dams, and channels of our inland waterways. They
spend about $670 million annually on this service, but in
1981 received back only $24 million in user fees. All this is a
subsidy for shipping interests. But do they need a subsidy?
No, they could pay higher user fees.

In 1981, vacationers paid entrance fees averaging about

3 cents each to use U.S. national parks, though it costs taxpayers $1.52 per visitor to keep up each of the 333 park sites. Thus, taxpayers footed the $443-million-a-year difference.

What's wrong with raising entrance fees a bit? At Grand Canyon National Park, for instance, a family of four in one car could pay $5 rather than the present $2. That's still much lower than the $9.75 it would cost that same family to ride the elevator up the Empire State Building to the observation deck. Raising entrance fees modestly at some twenty-five major Federal parks would bring in almost $11 million a year. Another $10 million could be raised by charging small fees at the twenty-three parks that are now free; by extending the collection hours at fourteen other parks; and by raising the price of the Golden Eagle Passport, which entitles the holder to unlimited use of all parks, to a modest $25. Back in 1916, it cost $8 per carload to get into Yosemite National Park, and $10 for Yellowstone. That $8 fee in 1916 is equivalent to a $65 fee today, and the $10 fee is equivalent to $83. So in truth, these fees have fallen substantially over the years.

The Forest Service gives away firewood—loads of it. More than four million cords of timber were given away in 1981 alone. That's equivalent to 11.2 million barrels of oil, worth $336 million dollars if you figure it at $30 a barrel. Between 1974 and 1980, permits to take the free firewood increased fivefold. What is the social purpose served by giving away the firewood? Why not charge for it?

Well, at one time there *was* a social purpose. Until 1973, only people who lived in or near a national forest got free firewood. Everyone else paid the going rate. But in 1973, when the oil crisis hit, the government decided to give out firewood so we wouldn't freeze. Yet as the oil crisis faded, the demand for free firewood only soared. From 1972 to 1980, demand for it rose by 1,100 percent. The government hasn't changed its policy to reflect the changed circumstances.

156

This type of situation occurs repeatedly throughout government. A need is identified and a program to address that need is established. The program increases in size as more people take advantage of the benefits offered. As the program expands, many who were never intended to be "helped" come to rely on what they see as their "right" to a government handout. Further, as time passes, the need for the program changes. The government is unable to (or won't) reevaluate the need for the program based on the current environment. So, spending continues to increase, with inefficiencies, waste, fraud, and abuse adding to costs.

The Freedom of Information Act requires that government agencies release government documents to the public unless there is some extremely defensible reason not to. But digging out the old files costs money. So in 1981, for example, the Food and Drug Administration alone processed 33,000 requests at a cost of $4.5 million. But the agency collected only $231,000 in fees for this service—slightly more than 5 percent of the tab. The rest was paid by taxpayers.

Now you will say, sure, why shouldn't the taxpayers subsidize all those crusading journalists and worried physicians who make the requests in the interests of our health? Right, except that more than 80 percent of the Freedom of Information requests came not from Ralph Nader and his legions but from the marketing departments of pharmaceutical companies doing routine studies on their competitors.

The total unrecovered cost of government publications was about $1.3 billion in fiscal 1982. This happens because various regulations and legislation set forth nearly one hundred years ago prohibit the government from charging adequate prices for the books and pamphlets it produces. Even modest price increases on Federal publications could raise $80–$100 million a year. In fact, Government agencies do not set the price on the publications they produce. Instead, the Government Printing Office sets price, handles sales, and collects revenues. All the GPO tries to recover is the actual "printing" cost of government publications, not their total production cost, which would include writing, editing, design, and typesetting.

We learned about the GPO up close. Our conclusions and recommendations were summarized in a book titled *War on Waste*, which sells for $9.95. The interesting point is that the GPO was selling that summary for $19.00. This price variance becomes more understandable once you know that a GPO pressman earns $17.53 an hour versus $13.33 in the private sector, and a bookbinder, $16.68 versus $12.77.

In fact, in 1982, GPO salaries were, on average, 42 percent higher than wages paid to other Federal workers in comparable positions. A proofreader in the GPO earns $30,252 a year versus $12,473 in Executive Branch agencies—$17,779, or 2.4 times more. Explains a lot, doesn't it?

Sales of the National Oceanic and Atmospheric Administration's nautical maps and charts in fiscal 1982 covered only 36 percent of costs. That represented a $40 million annual subsidy to the owners of airplanes, ships, and pleasure boats—none of whom seem particularly suitable candidates for governmental largess.

If all our recommendations to increase user charges and to have the government rely more on the private sector were implemented, the government could save $47.9 billion over three years. Not only is that a lot of taxpayer money (all the income taxes paid in one year by 21.6 million median-income American families), but the services we would get would improve enormously.

Chapter 10

What We Can Do

The Dangerous Game

It has become politically fashionable to decry the government's massive deficits. While Republicans and Democrats alike play "pin the deficits on the opposition," the underlying cause of those deficits—the uncontrolled growth in Federal spending—is largely ignored.

It is a dangerous game the politicians are playing. The stakes are the futures of our children and grandchildren. While the politicians play their games and the media keep score, our attention is diverted from the causes of the problem to the symptoms. Each time you read a newspaper, hear a radio broadcast, or watch a television show that discusses Federal deficits, you're not getting the whole story. This is because politicians don't want the full story told, and the media don't know what story to tell.

The deficit, again, is simply the difference between the amount of money that comes in and the amount of money that goes out. So the cause of increasing deficits should be straightforward and obvious—either we're taking in too little or we're spending too much.

To come up with an answer, let's compare 1962 and 1983. Nineteen sixty-two was generally considered to be a pretty good year for the United States. It was the first full year of the Kennedy Administration—a time of peace and prosperity. Inflation was 1.8 percent and the prime interest rate was 4.5

159

percent. Federal revenues were 18.2 percent of GNP while Federal spending was 19.5 percent. The difference between revenues and spending resulted in what would now be considered a minute deficit of $7.1 billion.

But in 1983, Federal revenues had risen to 18.6 percent of GNP, and spending was 24.7 percent of GNP. The result was a 1983 deficit of $195 billion, or more than twenty-seven times the 1962 deficit. Why? Clearly not because we're taxed any less today. Quite the contrary. The reason is that the government now spends much, much more.

If our current policies are continued, by the year 2000 Federal, state, and local spending will consume about one-half of this country's total output of goods and services. And *consume* is the key word since government spending produces very little.

Government spending is big and growing, but is that necessarily bad?

It is if you want a future for yourself, your children, and your grandchildren. A future in which you can look forward to more than higher taxes, higher inflation, higher interest rates, and higher unemployment. A future in which the government can no longer spend first and ask questions later. In other words, a future that preserves the values of our social and economic system.

But that's not the future we'll get if we don't control the government's fiscally profligate spending and force our political leaders to act more responsibly.

Once the fundamental problem is recognized as Big and Growing Government, there are three possible actions that we, as a country, can take: ignore it, cover it up, or fix it.

We *ignore* the problem by allowing the government to continue the use of 332 incompatible accounting systems that hide more than they show, are understood by very few, provide virtually no management control, and would quickly lead any business or individual into bankruptcy.

160

We *cover up* the problem by convincing the media to focus on a symptom, the deficit, rather than the cause, the runaway growth in government spending. Not recognizing the problem for what it is makes it very easy for politicians to argue for higher taxes, masking the symptom and allowing the government's continued growth.

We can *fix* the problem, but that will require hard decisions. Decisions that won't get any easier and that can't be postponed indefinitely. Decisions that must be made if our future isn't to be held hostage to the government's voracious appetite to tax and tax, spend and spend.

Now You See It, Now You Don't

The government's accounting and budgeting systems are just about useless as a means of controlling costs. The Federal budget itself is a political statement, not a financial document, and bears only a vague resemblance to similarly titled documents in the private sector. The accounting system—a true misnomer since little accountability is provided—makes it easy to ignore the growth in government spending since most officials don't even know what's actually being spent. In particular:

- The government doesn't know how much cash it has available and so needlessly incurs interest expense by unnecessary borrowing. For example, student loans are made before the beginning of the school year and before tuition payments are due. This has given enterprising students the opportunity to invest their student loans in interest-bearing accounts until the money is needed—an investment "financed" by the taxpayers since the government, in effect, borrows the money the students are investing. Conversely, the government lets cash seized from criminals sit idly in non-interest-bearing accounts.

161

- The government, with between $800 billion and $900 billion in outstanding loans and guarantees, doesn't know how much is current, how much is delinquent, how much is at subsidized interest rates, and so forth.

Let's take two specific examples involving the Rural Electrification Administration (REA) and the Farmers Home Administration (FmHA).

REA lends money to utilities in rural areas at a maximum interest rate of 5 percent. This is, of course, money that the government has to borrow at about 12 percent. Not surprisingly, REA is going broke, and the House of Representatives recently approved a $19-billion bailout plan.

Back in 1935, REA made sense. America was in the midst of a depression, and only about 10 percent of rural America had electric power. Today, rural America is "electrified" with 99 percent of farms with electricity. Now it would seem logical that there would be no need for REA today. Not true. Bureaucrats and their Congressional supporters have developed new activities to perpetuate REA. In the last ten years, taxpayers (that's you and me) have provided $70 billion in subsidies to rural electric cooperatives through REA's lending activities. "Rural electric cooperatives" have become giant utility companies subsidized by taxpayers.

Why are we making 5 percent loans to giant utilities for which the taxpayers are paying 12 percent interest? Ten million households make up a powerful special interest, and Congress will continue and probably expand the subsidies provided through REA. If you are not from one of the fortunate ten million households benefiting from lower electric rates because of REA subsidies, why not visit our nation's capital where you can see your tax dollars hard at work in the "rural" communities of Washington, D.C.?

If you ask someone in Congress—almost anyone in Congress—how much FmHA is spending, they'll get it wrong.

Why? The government's accounting procedures almost guarantee that they'll get it wrong.

For example, in just one program, the Agricultural Credit Insurance Fund, total spending is estimated to be about $13.5 billion in 1984. Congress, however, was asked to approve spending of only $1.5 billion, or a little more than one-tenth of actual spending.

Are you confused? Your Congressman would be too. Do you want to know how the government can spend nine times the amount authorized by Congress?

Well, it's magic, and if an individual or a corporation tried it, they'd probably end up in jail. But the government is a master of sleight-of-hand and can accomplish this particular bit of hocus-pocus largely by selling itself about $7 billion in loans. You see, the government spends money in two ways: "on-budget" and "off-budget." The "on-budget" items are included in the Federal budget, while "off-budget" items are not and therefore receive little attention from Congress. The "on-budget" Agricultural Credit Insurance Fund makes a loan and sells it to the "off-budget" Federal Financing Bank, which is required by law to buy the loan. Poof—the money is gone from the Federal budget. Houdini would be proud, and Congress and the American public are never fully informed of actual spending.

The Information Gap, or What You Don't Know Can Hurt You

As it is structured, the Federal budget, and the accounting systems underlying it, are a joke—a bad joke on the taxpayers, who deserve better. Information essential to Federal operations is either unavailable or is incomplete, inaccurate, or out of date. While enormous quantities of data are generated, usable information is hard to come by. The computer systems in just one agency, the Air Force Logistics

Command, generate six million pounds of paper per year—a lot of paper, but not much information.

And this lack of information is repeated tens of thousands of times throughout government. For example:

- The Social Security Administration has 138 million income items, valued about $89 billion, which cannot be assigned to specific accounts.
- The Urban Mass Transportation Administration has $25 billion in active, ongoing grants, yet has been unable to reconcile its accounts since 1977.
- The Veterans Administration pays $15 billion per year to six million claimants, of which it is known over $500 million is paid in error, but there is no formalized method to identify and correct problem areas.

Before you can fix something, you have to recognize it's broken, and the "Information Gap" makes it very difficult to identify and very easy to ignore the causes of the government's precarious financial condition.

The Great Cover-Up: "Tax the Rich" and Other Political Slogans

To understand the causes of the uncontrolled growth in Federal spending, you have to understand a basic truth: Nobody has ever been reelected for not spending. So, politicians love to spend money and, except before elections, they love to raise taxes, since that gives them more money to spend. The politician's answer to "runaway Federal spending" is "runaway Federal taxation."

The conventional wisdom of Washington's iron triangle of legislators, bureaucrats, and special interests views reductions in Federal spending as politically unthinkable—perhaps a slower rate of growth, but certainly not real cuts.

With our huge deficits, and the prospect of more of the

same, why do we allow the expenditure of staggering sums to benefit special interest groups to the detriment of the general public?

First, special interest groups are concentrated, coherent, and well organized, and they fight effectively to protect their benefits. Conversely, the general public is diffuse, unorganized, and ineffective in expressing and protecting its interests. Second, each concession to individual special interests costs relatively little, but the cumulative costs have resulted in the government's consumption of ever larger shares of the economic pie—consumption financed by increased taxation of the general public.

Raising taxes doesn't solve the underlying problem, it merely covers it up—deficits can be reduced by increased taxation, but inevitable new deficits will result from the continuing growth of government.

It can be politically very attractive to engage in this cover-up as, for example, a Presidential candidate calling for taxes on the rich to eliminate the deficit. Unfortunately, this is a cruel hoax on American taxpayers.

As I mentioned before, if we define as rich everyone with taxable income of $75,000 or more, and take everything above $75,000 not already taxed—not just tax it, but take it all— we'd get enough to run the government for about ten days. Obviously, this is no solution, and, even if it were, such confiscatory taxation would quickly force more—lots more— people into the underground economy, which is already costing us $100 billion a year in lost taxes.

In the United States, 90 percent of all taxable income is accounted for in brackets up to the $35,000 level. At higher income levels, there's just not enough income generated to appreciably reduce the deficit.

If we want to raise a significant amount of taxes, we have to go where the money is—to the lower- and middle-income taxpayers.

165

The median family income has increased from $3,187 in 1948 to $24,100 in 1983. Meanwhile, its tax burden has increased from $9 to $2,218. (Including Social Security taxes, the family's tax burden has increased from $39 in 1948 to $3,833 in 1983.) In other words, while its income has increased 7.6 times, its income taxes have gone up 246.4 times. And to balance the Federal Budget, we'd almost have to double this tax burden.

The problem is too much Federal spending, and neither ignoring it nor covering it up will make it go away.

2,478 Hard Solutions for Difficult Problems

The Federal government is the nation's largest borrower, lender, employer, insurer, land-owner, tenant, and landlord. It is responsible for the medical care received by 47 million people each year and provides 95 million subsidized meals each day.

The government is big and poorly run. That's why:

- The Pentagon purchases 3-cent screws for $91, 25-cent compressor caps for $100, 9-cent batteries for $114, and 60-cent light bulbs for $511.
- To construct facilities, the Veterans Administration spends twice as much per hospital bed and four times as much per nursing home bed as the private sector. Veterans Administration average hospital stays are three times those of the private sector, and medical claim *processing* costs are $100 to $140 per claim versus a $3 to $6 cost for private insurers.
- Fully half of the government's computers are obsolete with an average age twice that of those in the private sector. They are so old that manufacturers no longer service them, and the government spends $1 billion over three years just for the personnel to maintain them.

166

- The General Services Administration employs seventeen times as many people and spends almost fourteen times as much to manage its facilities as a comparable private-sector firm.
- There's a 41 percent delinquency rate on amounts owed the government. Little wonder since in the Department of Housing and Urban Development only three attempts are made to collect its delinquent accounts versus twenty-four to thirty-six attempts by private sector lenders.
- Military and Civil Service retirees receive from three to six times the total lifetime pension benefits of their private-sector counterparts. The government's pension benefits are so generous that it would take $450 billion annually for the private sector to provide comparable benefits—about three times the pretax profits of all nonfinancial U.S. companies.

This list goes on and on, but the point is obvious: waste and inefficiency abound in virtually every governmental operation. From the billion-dollar-a-year error rates on food stamps to the millions of dollars needlessly spent because the Department of Health and Human Services involves sixty people and takes an average of forty-seven days to respond to a single letter—waste and inefficiency are everywhere in government.

Rather than ignoring or covering up the problem of excessive government spending, we can "fix it" by identifying and eliminating waste and inefficiency.

Remember the bleak forecast outlined in chapter 1— a budget deficit of $2 trillion facing us in the year 2000, just a short sixteen years away? And this huge deficit despite massive increases in personal income taxes—an ironclad guarantee of permanent recession?

We are not alone in having recognized the precariousness of our nation's financial condition. Many analysts have stated that the Federal deficits threaten our economic vitality. Some have even correctly identified Federal spending as the cause of our economic problems and called for budgetary cuts. Unfortunately, those calls for spending cuts are usually presented in vague and general terms. It's almost as easy to say "cut the budget" as it is to say "raise taxes." The hard part is saying where the budget should be cut, whose "entitlement" will be eliminated. And we all feel "entitled" to something from the government, whether it's the rich yacht owner receiving free Coast Guard towing service or the defense contractor charging $436 for a $7 hammer—we'll all take something for nothing. Only it's not "something for nothing." We're paying with our taxes, and most of us just aren't getting our money's worth.

Rather than meaningless and unactionable calls to "cut the budget," the President's Private Sector Survey has recommended 2,478 specific ways to cut spending. From some of the major recommendations summarized in this book to the many hundreds of straightforward, commonsense improvements detailed in our forty-seven reports, our purpose was to reduce waste and inefficiency in government.

The total savings from full implementation of our recommendations would be $424.4 billion over three years.

A logical question is: What is the Administration doing to implement the recommendations of PPSS?

Through May 1984, the Administration either implemented or was in the process of implementing 636 of our recommendations, with three-year savings of $97.8 billion. For example:

- Reform of the Railroad Retirement System, including increased employee contributions, reduced taxpayer subsidies, and other measures to improve solvency. Savings: $2.4 billion over three years.
- Reduction in the backlog of Federal Tax Delinquencies by

improved staff utilization and establishing case priorities. Savings: $2.7 billion over three years.

- Accelerated deposit of Social Security taxes by state and local governments. Savings: $1.7 billion over three years.

These are only a few examples of what's being done, and much more work remains. But there is a limit to what the Administration can do to implement our recommendations.

There are three powers absolutely essential to running an organization, business, or government:

- Power to establish the organization structure,
- Power to set pay scales and incentives, and
- Power to control spending.

Then, you're in control.

The President has none of these powers—they reside in Congress.

Seventy-three percent of PPSS's recommendations require direct Congressional action, and most, if not all, of the remaining recommendations will be influenced by Congress. Even straightforward operating decisions have been subject to Congressional action. For example, Congress has written into law that the military is prohibited from obtaining competitive bids on the shipment of household goods to Alaska and Hawaii. This must benefit someone, but it's not the 10,445 median-income families whose taxes are wasted as they all go to pay for this senseless restriction.

Over and over, we have found it is Congressional policy to keep open unneeded, underutilized facilities, to retain unneeded employees, to pay duplicate benefits under a number of subsidy programs, to force the expenditure of taxpayer dollars on inefficient procurement practices—and the list goes on and on.

What can we do? We can demand that Congress grant the President the same power as that enjoyed by the governors of

169

forty-three states—the item veto. This simply means that if the President disagrees with a *part* of a bill, he can veto that part without vetoing the entire bill. Congress often includes items in bills that have no direct relations to the bills in which they are included. These unrelated items are called "riders" since they merely ride along with the main bill. For example, there could be language specifying that an unneeded military base will be maintained or that an unnecessary weather station will be kept open. If these "riders" were included in a multibillion-dollar agriculture appropriations bill, the only way the President could stop the rider is by vetoing the entire bill.

The U.S. Conference of Mayors summed it up with this resolution:

Whereas, the Congress frequently amends important and necessary legislation to include wasteful special-interest spending items; and whereas, the deficit problem cannot be solved while this irresponsible practice continues . . .

Clearly, our best chance at restoring fiscal sanity is the Presidential item veto. To quote San Francisco Mayor Dianne Feinstein:

It's in the best interest of the nation to have a strong executive, and to be able to hold that executive accountable, I think the line item veto clearly restores that responsibility.

It was once noted that democracy could not succeed, since inevitably the citizens would discover that they held the keys to the Treasury and would bankrupt the nation. Well, it hasn't been the American public that has made this discovery, but rather their elected representatives. They've taken us to the verge of bankruptcy—perhaps beyond—and still they promise more.

We have the best, most envied form of government in the world. It is so, precisely because it does finally respond to the will of the people. It often does so only after public pressure has reached a crescendo. But at least it does respond.

So, now I call on you to make an effort. It won't take much: an hour to sit and write a thoughtful letter. A few minutes to make a phone call to your Congressman. Here are some easy but effective things to do:

- Write a letter to your representatives, explaining that you want them to reduce government spending and stop the needless expenditure of your hard-earned tax dollars.
- Write a letter to the editor of the local newspaper, as well as national newspapers and magazines, expressing your views on wasteful government spending.
- Arrange for a speaker from the President's Private Sector Survey on Cost Control to address your trade association, service club, political organization, or taxpayer group.
- Spread the word about the information in this book. Grass roots support is essential if government spending is to be brought under control.

By taking action as an individual citizen, voter, and taxpayer, you reject the fashionable cynicism that says that the American democracy is no longer workable, that everyone is only out for himself, that patriotism is no more than a hollow flag-waving.

If we do nothing about the growth of government, we can be absolutely sure that the prosperity we have become accustomed to will fade very quickly. Now, if that doesn't send you running for your writing paper, then I don't know what will.

More than ever, we need the support of concerned taxpayers. Since many of our recommendations require Congressional action, it would be most helpful if you could write, call, and challenge your representatives in Washington, urging them to support PPSS recommendations.

171

No, we haven't come up with easy solutions to hard problems. But the solutions don't get any easier by ignoring the problem—by covering it up with tax increases and counterproductive, short-term savings that result in long-term costs.

Remember that Congressional instinct is to spend, never to save. We need to administer shock treatment to our elected representatives and let them know that their continued fiscal irresponsibility can no longer be tolerated. Much like the character in the movie *Network*, we're asking you to join with us in telling them that "We're mad as hell, and we're not going to take it anymore!"

Waste and Abuse from A to Z

ACTION   In fiscal year 1983 the ACTION Agency incurred almost $26 million in administrative costs and disbursed $92 million in grants for volunteer activities. That means 22 cents of every ACTION dollar was spent on administration versus 12 cents for the United Way.

Agricultural Credit Insurance Fund   This arm of the Department of Agriculture will spend $13.5 billion in fiscal 1984, but Congress approved only $1.5 billion, or 11.1 percent of that amount. The rest was hidden from scrutiny by various unbusinesslike accounting procedures employed throughout the Federal government.

Aid for Families with Dependent Children Program (AFDC)   Fifty percent of state administrative costs for this program are funded by the Federal government, regardless of cost. In fiscal 1981, the cost among states to administer an average monthly caseload ranged from $20 to $126, a 530 percent variance.

Automated Data Processing (ADP)   The average age of Federal computers is 6.7 years—already twice that in the private sector—and in five years will rise to an average of 10.1 years under current replacement plans. Currently, 50 percent of the government's computers are so obsolete that they are no longer serviced by their manufacturers and must be maintained by a specially trained staff at an added cost of $1.0 billion over three years.

Bidding for Spare Parts   The Air Force currently seeks competitive bids for less than 25 percent of its spare-parts purchases compared to 37 percent in 1973. If increased competition is brought into the procurement process at the Air Force, savings of $695 million over three years are achievable.

173

Bonneville Power Administration   This largest of the five Federal Power Marketing Administrations sells electricity for 2.45 cents per kilowatt hour—less than half the national average. Reflecting its low prices, between 1978 and 1982 Bonneville generated cash deficits between $500 million and $1 billion annually. Bonneville has also failed to meet its legal obligation to repay its Federal investment promptly.

Budgeting   Here are some examples of how the government manages to lose track of what it has spent, what it will spend or even how it thinks it should measure these amounts. Outlays are netted against related receipts, which means they are vastly understated. For example, if a loan program lends out $100 million this year, but takes in repayments of $50 million, reported outlays are only $50 million, even though actual spending this year is twice that amount. In measuring total outlays, the government leaves out certain agencies and operations arbitrarily, such as the Federal Financing Bank, as though these "off-budget" items did not even exist. Capital-outlay analyses are arbitrarily limited to three years; if a capital outlay is spread out over more than three years, complete data are impossible to obtain.

Cargo Preference Act   This law requires that 50 percent of Federal shipments by sea be carried on higher-cost U.S. flag vessels. Though the law was meant to maintain a modern merchant marine fleet, the average age of vessels participating in the program is twenty years. Its cost to the government is $605 million over three years.

Census Data   For the 1980 census, 37,000 clerks manually checked, edited, and accounted for 88 million questionnaires at a cost of $48.4 million, which was 45 percent over budget.

Civil Service Retirement System (CSRS)   CSRS's unfunded liability was $515 billion, as of September 30, 1982. If CSRS "reserved" for this liability using a 40-year amortization period, pension funding would amount to 85 percent of current CSRS payroll costs.

Commissaries   These military grocery stores were established in the 1800s to provide food supplies to servicemen in frontier areas at reasonable prices. Today, 238 domestic commissaries operate in such frontier areas as Washington, D.C. (six), San Diego (four), San Francisco (five), and Norfolk (four). The cost to taxpayers of domestic commissaries totaled $758 million in fiscal 1983.

174

Compensation The Social Security Administration (SSA) is attempting to modernize its computers. Even though SSA needs the best personnel available to accomplish this program, Federal pay for competent computer personnel is so out of line with the private sector that when SSA recently launched a recruiting drive to fill 600 positions, they received only a handful of applications. The result: high turnover and lengthy delays in getting the modernization program under way, which if accomplished would save taxpayers $8.6 billion over five years.

Contracting-out One of the major inefficiencies of government is that it tries to do everything: food service, maintenance, laundry, fire fighting, etc. These kinds of functions consume major portions of departmental and agency budgets and workforces. Contracting these functions out to the private sector could save $7.4 billion over three years.

Cost of Living Adjustments (COLAs) Military and civil service retirement plans are fully indexed to the consumer price index, a benefit virtually unheard of in the private sector. As a result of this benefit, an officer who retired in the early 1970s could be earning more from just his pension than an equally graded active officer earns in salary.

Davis-Bacon Act This law, enacted during the Depression in 1931 to protect the earning power of construction workers, is still on the books even though construction workers' average salaries exceed the average for all workers by approximately 50 percent. In part because of the law's complex requirements, local contractors— whom the law was passed to protect—are used in only 28 percent of projects where Davis-Bacon applies but in 47 percent where Davis-Bacon does not apply. Repeal of the Act would save the Government $4.97 billion over three years.

Debt Federal debt held by the public will total $1.3 trillion at the end of fiscal 1984, over $17,000 for every taxpayer. By the year 2000, if Federal policies remain unchanged, Federal debt will total over $13 trillion or an average of over $50,000 for every man, woman, and child currently living in the United States.

Debt Collection About 95 percent of the total recorded debt owed to the Federal government is managed by 24 different agencies. A lack of uniformity of methods and definitions—both among and within these agencies—impedes debt monitoring and collection. Since collections are turned in to the Treasury and do not affect an

175

individual agency's appropriations, there is little incentive to improve the system.

Disaster Funds   The Congress generally funds Federal disaster relief programs in advance by making annual lump-sum appropriations to agency disaster accounts. This advanced funding does not earmark funds for a specific disaster and thus the agencies can allocate funds at their own discretion. In 1980, Congress made $946 million available as a reactive measure to aid in the Mount St. Helens disaster. Due to the phrasing of the regulation, however, the money could be used in other areas. In fact, only $386 million of the $946 million (41 percent) had been spent on the Mount St. Helens disaster. The balance of $560 million was ostensibly spent on other disasters though it could not be traced because it "lost its identity."

Dual Pay for Active Reserve Duty   Eighty-four percent of private sector employees who are also members of the Reserves or National Guard receive pay differentials from their regular employers while on active duty. That means most private sector corporations pay the difference between military pay and the employee's regular pay, so that the total equals the regular job's compensation. The Federal government, however, grants full pay plus compensation for active duty.

Dual Sourcing   After a weapons manufacturer wins a contract from the military—usually by "under-bidding" with unrealistically low amounts—the manufacturer becomes the sole source for twenty years, at which time costs are typically doubled and tripled in the absence of competition. By maintaining at least two competitive sources the President's Private Sector Survey on Cost Control estimates annual savings of approximately $340 million.

Early Retirement   Early retirement in the private sector means reduced retirement benefits. In the government, however, the reductions in benefits for early retirees are not as significant. In the private sector benefits are reduced an average 4.5 percent for each year below age 62 one retires early. In the government it is less than half the penalty or an average of 2 percent for each year below the age of 55.

Electronic Funds Transfer   The government pays bills 10.2 days earlier than necessary on average and its total procurement costs are estimated at about $175 billion per year, or about $480 million per day. Using electronic funds transfer to keep funds in interest-

176

bearing accounts for as long as possible would save the government $7.0 billion over three years.

Entitlement Programs   The Census Bureau reported that in 1981, one out of six of the nation's 85.5 million households received one or more of the following needs-based benefits: food stamps, school lunch, public housing, and Medicaid.

Excess Sick Leave   A Federal worker is permitted to save up his sick days without limit, then add the unused days onto total service for the purpose of calculating retirement annuities. This benefit is not found in the private sector. Discontinuing this costly practice would save taxpayers $1.1 billion over three years.

Farmers Home Administration (FmHA)   This arm of the Department of Agriculture exists to suppy credit as a last resort to the farm sector. However, 70 percent of the borrowers loaned money by the FmHA are not farmers. The delinquency rate among these nonfarm borrowers is 26 percent, more than seven times the private-sector average of 3–4 percent even though the average interest rate on these loans is only 2.7 percent.

Feeding Expenditures   The government spent $26.7 billion in fiscal 1981 on all its feeding programs, providing 95 million subsidized meals each day—enough to feed everyone in the thirty-one largest cities in America three square meals per day.

Firewood Program   The government gave away $235 million of firewood in 1981, an amount equal to 24.5 percent of total commercial harvest in that year.

Food Stamps   Food stamp fraud and abuse is estimated at $1 billion annually—an amount equal to the income taxes paid by 450,857 median-income families. The formula used to calculate food stamp benefits has not changed since 1971 even though the characteristics of the average family receiving food stamps have changed—benefits could be reduced by 35 percent while still meeting original nutritional goals.

Foreign Military Sales   The Department of Defense (DOD) continues to subsidize foreign military sales programs by not charging foreign governments the estimated replacement costs of equipment and spare parts sold from inventory. Three main weaknesses were identified in defense pricing policies: (1) inflation factors used to estimate replacement costs were unrealistically low; (2) inflation factors were not compounded when items were purchased more than one year prior to their sale; and (3) the Air Force

177

and Navy normally updated prices only once per year. This led to millions of dollars of lost revenue. For example, at one Air Force Logistics Center studied, fiscal 1980 sales of $43 million were underpriced by $17 million.

Foreign Service Retirement System (FSRS) Costs of the Foreign Service Retirement System ($372 million in fiscal year 1983) are equal to 93 percent of payroll costs, 3.2 times the comparable costs of the Civil Service Retirement System, and 7.5 times comparable private-sector levels.

Grazing Fees The grazing fees charged by the National Park Service (NPS) are about 20 percent of the rates obtained on private grazing land. NPS would have to raise its fees 2.5 times just to cover the cost of administering the grazing lands and would still be charging only about one-half the private-sector rate.

Guaranteed Student Loans Because of poor collection practices the default rate on guaranteed student loans is estimated at 8.0 percent in 1984, or a total of $2.4 billion. In 1982, an investigation uncovered 46,860 current and retired Federal employees holding defaulted student loans with a combined value of $68 million. Consolidating student loan programs and making other management improvements would save the government $2.445 billion over three years.

Health Benefits Private-sector health plans cost an average of $93 per month per family, one-third lower than the Federal health-plan average cost of $134 per family. As a portion of payroll, the average is 5.8 percent in the private sector, 6.8 percent in the government. This seemingly slim one-percentage-point difference between government and private health-plan costs represented $358 million in extra outlays for taxpayers in 1981. Bringing the average in line with private-sector experience would save taxpayers $1.4 billion over three years.

Health Care The Federal share of total U.S. health care expenditures doubled between 1965 and 1975, rising from 13.1 percent to 27.9 percent. Over that same period, total health care spending grew 1.5 times faster than GNP. By 1995 under current policies the Medicare trust fund will have run a cumulative deficit of $300 billion.

Health Professions and Nursing Student Loan Program A computer check of delinquent Health Professions and Nursing

Student Loan borrowers identified 690 doctors and nurses—who collectively owed $490,000—as government employees. An additional 28 individuals owing a total of $22,000 were coordinating research projects under grants awarded by the National Institutes of Health.

Horrible An appropriate adjective to describe the current management of the Federal government. To change this situation, PPSS recommended the creation of an Office of Federal Management which would create and consolidate the functions that can be found in the headquarters of all successful major corporations, such as financial management, budgeting, personnel management, etc.

Hospital Construction Costs The Veterans Administration Hospital in the Bronx cost $153,000 per bed or 1.6 times the $97,400 per bed spent constructing the comparable Duke University Hospital.

Household Goods When military personnel have been transferred to destinations outside North America and need to move household goods to their new locations, the Military Traffic Management Command (MTMC) normally solicits competitive bids from household-goods-moving contractors. However, if the household goods are to be moved to either Alaska or Hawaii, competitive bidding is prohibited due to restrictive language in DOD appropriations legislation. This holds in spite of a study during 1977 that showed that the use of competitive bidding reduced moving rates an average of 26.0 percent on household goods moved to Alaska and 20.5 percent on household goods moved to Hawaii. If the DOD solicits competitive bids for movement of household goods to Alaska and Hawaii, it could save $69.5 million over three years.

Incentive Funds Incentive funds are used to correct critical manpower shortages in the National Guard and other Reserve units. Although funds for the incentive program increased fourfold between fiscal year 1979 and fiscal year 1982, the Army has not determined the effectiveness of the incentives in assisting recruiting and retention. Thus, the Army has spent $110 million over a three-year period without knowing whether any benefit was achieved.

Incompatible Computer Equipment The government spends $12 billion a year on computers. However, practically no consideration is given to whether the new computers that are purchased are compatible—able to communicate—with the computers the government already owns. In New York alone, the regional office of Health and Human Services uses ten different brands of incompatible computers.

Insurance Programs   As of September 30, 1982, the Federal government had issued insurance coverage totaling $2.1 trillion, against which it had accumulated reserves sufficient to cover only 1.0 percent of potential claims. PPSS found that Federal insurance premiums did not adequately cover the risk and costs of the programs and that coverage could be more efficiently provided by the private sector.

Inventory Management   The Department of Defense orders needlessly large quantities of goods and equipment to create volume discounts, but this practice increases inventory costs. In the DOD these extra costs often more than offset the savings publicized with respect to the large-volume discounts. Balancing these costs and benefits against one another in the interest of optimal efficiency is a standard practice in the private sector. Instituting such a system in the government procurement process could save taxpayers $3.5 billion on a one time basis and another $1 billion over three years.

Judges   Administrative law judges overturn 60 percent of the Social Security disability cases that are appealed to them because they base their decisions on criteria different from what is used at lower levels in the disability system. Reforming the Social Security disability appeals system could save $3.6 billion over three years.

Key Personnel   Because retirement benefits are so generous in the Federal government more employees are retiring as soon as possible; 65 percent of eligible employees retired in 1980 versus 20 percent in 1978. From 1977–1981, the government's executive pay ceiling rose 5.5 percent whereas Federal pensions increased 55 percent during the same period, a strong incentive to retire and a major reason the government is losing its key people at an accelerating rate.

Ladder Climbing   For some professional occupations the timelapses between promotions in the government are about 40 percent shorter than the wait in the private sector, and each promo-

180

tion comes with a raise averaging 40 percent more than the one you would get working outside government.

Lease Negotiations   The General Services Administration (GSA) leases property for government agencies. GSA requires an average of 366 days to complete a lease negotiation, even though GSA has announced the "goal" of reducing that time-frame to 283 days. Slow negotiations cost money, because real-estate prices can rise $.50 to $2.50 per square foot in the time GSA takes to negotiate. In the private sector, the average lease is negotiated in 180 days, about half the time it takes the government.

Length of Hospital Stays   The average stay in a VA hospital is 21 days, nearly three times the private-sector average of 7.2 days. This disparity costs taxpayers $1.6 billion annually.

Letter Answering   A single response to correspondence requiring the signature of the Health and Human Services Secretary involves 55–60 people and takes 47 days to complete. The VA requires 20 days. In the private sector, the president of the Chamber of Commerce of the U.S. responds to correspondence in five days.

Medical Claims Processing   It costs the Veterans Administration about $100–$140 to process (not pay) one medical claim. The average among private insurance and other fiscal intermediaries is $3–$6 per claim.

Micromanagement   Congress requires its approval on each property worth more than $1,000 disposed of by the GAO. By comparison, the boards of directors of many large corporations permit senior management to sell assets worth $1 million without specific approval.

Military Bases   Of 4,000 Defense Department installations in the U.S. only 312 are considered significant; the rest are support facilities with fewer than 150 employees each. Congress has passed legislation to make closing unnecessary facilities a time-consuming, difficult process. Proposals to close certain installations announced in 1976 have still not been resolved, and no such announcements have been made since 1979. Potential savings of $2 billion annually would be realized if military-installation realignment and consolidation efforts were completed.

Military Pensions   The law requires reserves to be set aside in the private sector for future pension obligations. Applying such a standard to military pensions reveals $527 billion in unfunded liabilities, an increase of $171 billion in three years or an unfunded

181

future liability growth of $57 billion annually from 1979–1982. If 40-year amortization principles were applied to military pensions the reserve requirements and current costs would amount to 118 percent of base pay whereas the corresponding figure for private-sector plans is approximately 14 percent.

Mortgage Loans   The General Accounting Office (GAO) found that most subsidized mortgage loans in 1982 were not made to low- and moderate-income households in need of assistance, but rather to those who could have purchased homes without assistance. The typical mortgage revenue bond homebuyer was an individual or two persons between 20 and 35 years of age with an income between $20,000 and $40,000. More than half of the subsidized borrowers were among the more affluent half of the families in their states, with some making over $50,000 annually.

Multiyear Procurement   Multiyear procurement involves negotiating volume discounts for things continually purchased. This system results in better utilization of the suppliers' facilities (who can spread their fixed costs out rather than calculating them each year), and a reduction in administrative burdens created by the current "stop-go" budget process.

National Direct Student Loans   The Department of Education is hampered in collecting defaulted National Direct Student Loans because of inadequate data submitted by the schools administering the loans. At least 55,000 or 23 percent of the 238,000 loans submitted before September 15, 1979, lacked original loan amounts and loan dates, amounts repaid, and the Social Security numbers of the borrowers.

National Parks   In 1981, visitors to the U.S. National Parks paid an average of about 3 cents each in entrance fees toward the $1.52-per-person cost of operating and maintaining the 333 park sites. Taxpayers footed the rest of the bill, which totaled $452.8 million.

Nonfiling Taxpayers   Some individuals avoid taxes by simply not filing a return. About 5 million people, owing some $2 billion in income taxes, did not file returns in 1972, the most recent year for which reliable data are available.

Nursing Home Construction   The VA spends $61,250 per bed to construct nursing homes versus $15,900 per bed for Beverly Enterprises, a national private-sector operator of nursing homes.

Obsolescence   The General Services Administration (GSA) esti-

182

mates that the government's computer acquisition process takes two and a half to four years. This means that it is virtually impossible for the government to keep pace with new developments in computers, since the computers are obsolete by the time they are acquired. In the private sector computers are upgraded every two to three years.

Office Space Utilization The Federal government is attempting to reduce its office space by 19 percent per person, from 167 square feet in 1982 to 135. They're acomplishing this goal at the rate of 2.5 square feet per person per year, meaning it will take thirteen years to achieve. The total potential savings for taxpayers comes to $11 million per square foot reduction, or $352 million annually if and when this result actually comes about.

On-the-job Injuries The Federal government reported that 6.3 percent of employees filed on-the-job claims in 1980. About half of these, 3.2 percent, lost time from work. Metropolitan Life Insurance Company reported that 1.7 percent of private-sector employees filed such claims, and only one-quarter of these, 0.42 percent, lost time from work.

Overgrading Under the General Schedule (GS) classification system in the Washington, D.C., area, nearly one-third of all positions are misclassified with the wrong grade, occupation, or title. Nationally, similar errors cost taxpayers $682 million annually.

Patent Applications The Patent and Trademark Office receives 20,000 pieces of mail a day. They are processed by an all-paper, hand-file and routing system. The backlog of patent applications awaiting review is now two years, having doubled over the past six years.

Payroll Checks The cost of issuing an Army payroll check is $4.20, more than four times the private-sector average of $1.00.

Physical Infrastructure The way to pay for roads, bridges, dams, and buildings is to have a long-term capital plan so the expenditures can be spread out. The government has seriously neglected this procedure, and as a result, local, state, and Federal governments are facing $2.5–$3 trillion in unplanned capital expenditures during this decade alone just to maintain today's deteriorated service levels.

Post Offices About one-third of all post offices, 12,469 of them, serve a hundred or fewer customers. The GAO has identified 7,067 of these as candidates for replacement with more economic facilities that would provide the same services at a savings of $272 million over three years. At the rate the Postal Service is following up on the GAO's recommendations, it should have all these consolidations accomplished by the year 2087, 103 years from now.

Property Management Compared to the property-management division of a large private-sector life insurance firm with management responsibility for comparable assets and facilities, the General Services Administration uses 17 times the number of administrative and professional personnel and has a total management cost that is 14 times greater.

Quality Control The Statistical Quality Control (SQC) system is the Veterans Administration's primary mechanism for measuring the accuracy of benefit payments—which totaled $16.4 billion for major programs alone in fiscal year 1982. However, the SQC system does not accurately measure the level of payment errors made. A nationwide Inspector General audit found error rates of 8.6 percent for education benefits and 5.4 percent for compensation benefits. These figures are two and three times higher than the rates determined by VA's own detection system.

Reduction in Force (RIF) Eight thousand Federal employees are receiving pay for jobs with higher grades than they actually perform. Reason: Current RIF procedures provide that Federal employees retain their previous salary grade for two years if they are reduced to a lower-level position through no fault of their own. There are cases of $50,000 government executives reduced to clerical level who still receive $50,000. The 8,000 Federal employees receiving RIF compensation on this basis cost taxpayers $34 million annually.

Requests Under Freedom of Information Act (FOIA) Requesting FOIA material has become standard practice for private-sector market research—one pharmaceutical firm filed 1,250 requests in 1982 alone. Fees charged by Federal agencies to process these requests generally cover less than 10 percent of the costs associated with these activities and frequently recovery is less than 1 percent of costs.

"Shear" Waste Since 1954 when the Wool-Incentive Program was introduced, increased use of synthetic fibers and imported wool has greatly reduced the demand for domestic wool—and also the need for the program. Nonetheless, in 1980 the government spent $42.1 million on the program, increasing wool output by between 7 and 16 million pounds. In effect each additional pound—whose market value was about 88 cents—cost the government between $2.63 and $6.01.

Social Security Manual The Social Security System provides a manual to its claims processing personnel. The manual is large; if its 45,000 recipients stacked their copies atop one another the pile would be 34 miles high. Not only that, each recipient also receives 12,000 pages of annual revisions.

Social Security Payments The Social Security Administration (SSA) made $14.6 billion in erroneous payments from 1980–1982. Almost $1.3 billion is due to the failure of Old Age and Survivors Insurance beneficiaries to report their earnings. The system used by SSA to enforce proper income reporting is three years behind schedule, and the delay cost the government $128 million in interest for fiscal year 1983 alone.

Software Although less expensive alternatives exist for agencies procuring computer software, most choose to have their equipment custom-developed. In fact, 98 percent of the application software surveyed by the GAO had been custom-developed, adding both expense and time to the procurement process. One case that could have been reduced through consolidated or "off-the-shelf" buying is that of payrolling software.

Standard Accounting Practices Despite a law requiring the GAO to establish standard accounting principles across all agencies, there are three hundred different automated accounting systems which use incompatible methods among the various Federal agencies. One result is massive duplication in the development of agency software; another is that no one seems to know what all these helter-skelter efforts taken together actually cost.

Supervision The Department of Energy (DOE) has twice the number of supervisors per employee than the Federal government as a whole—one supervisor for every three employees versus one for seven government-wide.

Supplemental Security Income (SSI) Program Overpayments under the SSI program for fiscal year 1981 totaled more than $400 million, an average overpayment of $105 per recipient.

Tax Examination By 1981 noncompliance with Federal tax laws had doubled from its 1977 level and stood at $97 billion. It is expected to reach $133 billion by 1985. Despite growing non-compliance, the IRS has decreased its percentage of tax examinations from 2.4 percent of all filings in 1977 to 1.7 percent in 1983. This reduction in examinations equals 20 percent for the period 1977–1983.

Training   Due to variances in the number of Army recruits scheduled for training versus the number actually being trained, a large amount of unused capacity exists. The total waste in fiscal year 1981 alone was 26,600 training slots, with a total value of $169 million.

Travel   Federal travel expenses were $4.8 billion in fiscal year 1982. About $2.4 billion or 50 percent of the expenses were incurred at the full-fare rate although it is obvious that government business is large enough to earn discounts. Reason: no centralized travel procurement. Centralizing travel procurement, together with discount opportunities presented by fare deregulation, would save taxpayers $984 million over three years.

Turnover of Management   The average turnover for political appointees in Federal departments and agencies is eighteen months, and such tenure brevity results in a costly lack of management continuity. In the General Services Administration alone—an agency with 28,000 employees—there have been nine administrators, ten deputy administrators, and fourteen procurement commissioners in the past ten years.

Undersecured Loans   The 11,362 delinquent, emergency-disaster loans to farmers are undersecured by $1.1 billion, according to an estimate by the Office of the Inspector General. This is due to inadequate loan supervision and servicing, improper dispositions of loan security, declines in the value of farm capital, and the overstated values of crops. The Farmers Home Administration, which oversees the program, has compounded the problem by refinancing delinquent borrowers without providing required management assistance.

Uniform Services University of the Health Sciences (USUHS)
The Department of Defense established USUHS to train medical students to become military doctors. It costs $77,186 per year to train a student at USUHS as of fiscal year 1983 versus $19,146 through the Health Professions Scholarship Program (HPSP), the primary source of physicians for the military. There is no convincing evidence that further operation of USUHS is justified, and,

closing the facility would save taxpayers $117 million in three years.

Urban Discretionary Grants   Local transit authorities are unable to keep up with the flood of Federal grant money administered by the Urban Mass Transportation Administration (UMTA). A 1983 audit revealed nearly $1 billion in Federal rail modernization funds lying idle in transit authority offices. The UMTA has no formal documented system for the selection, approval, and awarding of urban discretionary grants.

Urban Mass Transportation Administration   Weaknesses in Federal accounting and control systems make it impossible for many departments and agencies to close their books, collect on delinquent accounts or remit accurate payments. The Urban Mass Transportation Administration (UMTA), for example, has spent $10 million on a computer, yet has been unable to close its books since 1979. This agency had a fiscal-year 1982 operating authority of $3.4 billion and controls $25 billion in active, ongoing grants.

Vacation Time   Federal government workers start accruing vacation days almost as soon as they get on the job. The typical Federal worker has already accumulated 6.5 days of vacation his first six months into the job whereas his private-sector counterpart gets only 4.8 days after six months. Not only that, the Federal worker starts accruing vacation days his third month into the job; private sector employees usually don't get any vacation until six to eleven months of service have passed. Altering Federal vacation policy to patterns found in the private sector would save taxpayers $3.8 billion over three years.

Vehicle Fleet Management   Excluding the Postal Service, the government has the world's largest fleet of nonmilitary vehicles with 318,000. Government vehicles are used an average of 9,000 miles per year, 64·percent less than the 25,000 per year considered optimal by private-sector rental companies. Because the government does not recondition vehicles prior to resale, the money lost at resale costs taxpayers $4 million annually.

Wastewater Projects   It takes two years to construct a wastewater project, but it takes the Federal government seven years to bring such a project from the planning stage to completion. The first five years are spent on red tape.

187

Waterways Programs   The Army Corps of Engineers and the TVA construct and maintain locks, dams, and channels that facilitate commercial traffic on inland waterways. Their fiscal-year 1981 spending for construction, operation, and maintenance was about $670 million. About $24 million, less than 4 percent, was collected from the businesses that used these waterways. The other 96 percent was paid by the taxpayers.

Weapons Systems Acquisition   Cost estimates for twenty-five major weapons systems initiated between 1971 and 1978 have increased 223 percent—from $105 billion at the outset to $339 billion as of 1981 estimates. Contractors for weapons typically "underbid" to get a foot in the door, then, contract signed (and competition cleared out of the way), work proceeds on the program and estimates are doubled and tripled. Of course, then it's too late to stop, and the taxpayers pay. Initial bids have been as much as 80 percent lower than final costs.

Wind Tunnel Charges   NASA charges $2,000 per hour for the use of its wind tunnel compared with the Defense Department's $6,000 charge for virtually the same service. The result is a disproportionate use of NASA wind tunnels and a substantial loss of revenue.

Xeroxed Copies of the PPSS Final Report   Something for which the Department of Commerce charged $45.95 on a break-even basis. The report was later made available by the Government Printing Office for $19, and finally the report was released in book form by a private-sector publisher, Macmillan Publishing Company, New York, for $9.95 per copy.

Yacht Owners   A wealthy group of individuals who are subsidized by the general taxpayer through the provision of free towing services by the Coast Guard in non-life-threatening situations.

Zero Freedoms   What U.S. citizens will have in the year 2000 when government debt totals $13 trillion—$169,000 per current taxpayer—and the annual Federal deficit reaches $2 trillion.

Index